THE
BREAKING
POINT

WHY NOT ME?
WHY NOT NOW?

MICHAEL DOW
FOREWORD BY DANIEL KOLENDA

Dedication

———⚬⚬⚬———

I dedicate this project to all of those who have given their life to the pursuit of God. I dedicate this book to those who have apprehended Him, and thus, cannot be settled or satisfied with lesser realities and attractions of this life. I dedicate this book to those hungry hearts that continue on after Jesus with great violence because they realize the significance of the day that they have been given to steward. I dedicate this book to all of you who know in your heart of hearts that God has broken into your life, and because of that, He is now breaking into a generation through your life! I commend you. I stand with you. Together, we are the breaking point!

Table of Contents

Acknowledgments

⸻⚬⚬⚬⸻

Thank you to everyone that helped to make this project such a great success. Thank you to Anna, my wife, for standing with me, believing in me, and contending with me for all that God has for our lives.

Thank you to my children, Ariyah, Josiah, and Emma, for allowing me to learn so much about life and love through you.

Thank you to Daniel Kolenda for writing the Foreword to this book. You have been my friend since the night Jesus found me. Your life is a great example of what it looks like when God breaks into the heart of a man, and how that man can change a generation. I honor you greatly.

Thank you to Dr. Robert Gladstone for your contribution to this work through video. I would not be who I am today if the Lord had not allowed me the privilege to be connected to you.

Thank you to Neil Broere, owner of Iron Kite Films, for doing such an incredible job putting together all of the videos for this book. Your dedication and diligence are second to none in filmmaking.

Thank you to Jim McMahel for creating an outstanding cover design. You are a great man of God and I am blessed to call you friend.

Thank you to Kathy Curtis for your time, effort, and amazing work in editing and typesetting; all of this could not have happened without you.

Thank you to Neil Broere, Founder of Iron Kite International and Fire Missionary; Eric Gilmour, of Sonship International; Brian Guerin, of Bridal Glory International; Michael Koulianos, of Jesus Image; David Popovici and Frankie Rodriguez, of Kingdom Gospel Mission, and Fabian Grech, Founder of Freedom to Captives, for your video contributions to this work. Thank you for being powerful men of God. Thank you for helping to give a fuller, more beautiful picture of Jesus to this generation.

Foreword

⸺⸺∞⸺⸺

Years ago I had a vision that I will never forget in which I saw a mighty, seemingly impenetrable dam. On one side was a great river and on the other was a desert, bone dry, parched, completely barren. In my vision I understood that the river represented the glory of God and the dry ground represented the world, perishing for want of it. I remembered the famous Scripture, "For the earth shall be filled with the knowledge of the glory of the LORD, as the waters cover the sea" (Hab. 2:14) but I could not see how it was possible. I said, *Lord how will the river breach that mighty wall?* And then I saw something amazing; tiny hairline fractures began to form in the dam. Razor sharp spirits of water were spraying through these tiny cracks. They seemed insignificant, but as time went on, the tremendous pressure of the water being forced through those fissures caused the cracks to grow and multiply. After a while, gaping holes opened in the wall allowing torrents of water to come rushing through. It was unstoppable! Then the inevitable happened. All of a sudden the wall gave way and the river completely reclaimed its territory. The dry ground was totally covered…"as the waters cover the sea."

Then the Lord showed me something remarkable. Man was created to usher God's dominion and glory into the world. Instead our stubborn natures and rebellious hearts have always resisted. We have become a wall, opposing God's will. But the Lord showed me those cracks in the wall were *people* through whom His glory was being channeled into the world. God wasn't just spontaneously pouring His presence into the earth. He was doing it the way He has always done it—through human agents. But where will God find such men?

I was immediately taken to the Last Supper where Jesus broke the bread of communion, gave it to His disciples and said, "This is my body which is broken for you" (1 Cor. 11:24). When He spoke of His "broken" body, He was referring to His crucifixion. Then I heard the words of the apostle Paul in Galatians 2:20, "I am crucified with Christ: nevertheless I live; yet not I, but Christ liveth in me: and the life which I now live in the flesh I live by the faith of the Son of God, who loved me, and gave himself for me." You see, Christ offers to us the cross, the instrument of brokenness. He invites us to be "broken" or "crucified" with Him because through that brokenness (the crucified life) His life is lived through us ("I am crucified with Christ, nevertheless I live; yet not I, but Christ liveth in me..."). This is how the wall is breached. This is how the river of God is breaking through.

> **What I am describing is nothing less than the Kingdom (the dominion) of God being channeled into the world in this age.**

What I am describing is nothing less than the Kingdom (the dominion) of God being channeled into the world in this age. The glory that will one day cover the whole earth is seeping in, even now, through the crucified lives of broken men and women. Jesus was the prototype and we are called to take up our cross and follow Him. This is not a burden. On the contrary, it is the highest form of living.

If you've met Michael Dow, you may find it hard to believe that this gentle, sweet-spirited lover of Jesus was once a thug. But I was there the night he met Jesus and I can testify to the amazing miracle that God has worked in his life since then. The Lord broke him down like a rancher breaks a wild stallion. Again and again I saw how Michael yielded to the Master. The man you see today is a changed man, a broken man, a crucified man. This is why the Lord uses Michael the way He does.

What has impacted me most about Michael's ministry is his willingness to be a "crack in the wall"—a "breaking point." He is a living example of what he preaches and teaches. I am sure that as you read what the Lord has given him on the following pages, you will receive grace to live a yielded and fruitful life, to be a "breaking point" for the Kingdom of God, in Jesus' name!

—Daniel Kolenda
President, Christ for All Nations
Evangelist and Author

Introduction

⟶ ∽∞∽ ⟶

Never has there been a more important day in the entire world than today. How could I dare say such a thing? For this reason, what happens today will determine the course the rest of your life will take. The decisions you make, or don't make, today will shape what you walk into tomorrow. That sounds like a pretty big deal, and it should, because it is.

We have one shot at this thing called life. There are no second chances. You can't go back at the end of your days and ask for a redo. For as many that would wish to hit the rewind button once they finally make it to their last days, it simply cannot be done. There is no magic formula. There is no special drink or pill. All we are left to be is what we decide to do in the moment, and then moment by moment, we are currently writing what will be known as the history of our lives.

What are you currently writing about your life? If your story were to be read aloud, what does your life have to say about you? Would it say things that you would want read aloud? Would it say things that you would be proud to stand up for? Would it say things that are having a profound effect upon the generation that you have been chosen to be alive in? I hope so. In fact, I pray so.

We have one shot at this thing called life. There are no second chances. You can't go back at the end of your days and ask for a redo.

This life that we have been given to live is precious. It is precious because it has been given to us as a gift. Not a single one of us scheduled our entrance into this world. We did not hand select our birthday. We were not able to sit down and study the world first in order to determine what region we would like to live in or what house and family we wanted to be a part of. Our life was carefully crafted before we ever even knew we would be a part of it. In Jeremiah chapter 1, God has this to say to the young prophet, "Before I formed you in the womb I knew you, and before you were born I consecrated you; I have appointed you as a prophet to nations."[1]

Why would I go to the Bible in order to make a point about our lives? Similar to the way that you

---

[1] Jer. 1:5, NASB

would consult the instruction manual with any electronic device that you were having an issue with, I turn to the Scriptures, God's instruction manual for our life, in order to find out the way that things should work. God is the great designer of life. God is the mastermind behind all that we know and see. God was at the beginning, and He too shall be found again at the end. But what about everything that is found in the middle?

Many are comfortable to say that God was at the beginning. Some are comfortable to say that God will again be found at the end. But what do you do with the middle portion of this life, as we know it? What do you do with the right now? How does God fit in to your right now? Is there a way for God to get in to your right now? My answer would be an ecstatic yes!

I would say that God does want in to your right now. But what does that look like? How does that even happen? Well, I am talking about more than just attending a church service, although I do believe that church services are necessary. Many are too comfortable with just going to a building once or twice a week and checking off their religious checklist that they have made time for God. Sadly enough, we think that God just wants some of our life, and so we create these little spiritual exercises that we perform on a regular basis in order to appease this Divine Being, when in reality God is not just trying to get in to a portion of my life…He wants it all!

Your life is not an accident. I don't know what you were told, or how you feel about it, but you are not here by mistake. It does not matter to me so much how you got here. Do not allow those details to drive the way you view your life. What does matter is that God said yes to you. God alone is the One who gives life, and He said yes to your life. In the same way that He told Jeremiah, He knew you before He knit you together in the womb. Don't place limitations on what your life can or can't be because of the details that got you here. Whatever had to happen in order for you to get here happened, and now that you are here, know this…it was not an accident; it was by design—divine design.

Whatever had to happen in order for you to get here happened, and now that you are here, know this…it was not be accident; it was by design— divine design.

Now, I am not saying that you are living in the fullest expression of what your life is supposed to be all about. This is where we come back to the importance of our decisions. However, in whatever way you are choosing to live right now there is hope; hope for a turnaround, hope for a different direction, hope for a changed outcome. Again, we've only got one shot at this thing, and my prayer for you is this: that with your one shot, you would make it count.

In my earlier days of walking with Jesus I received a wonderful challenge, an invitation if you would, from the Lord. I was in a period where I was attempting to find my way, trying to connect with what the purpose of my life was to be all about. It was during that time that I came across a small obscure little passage in the book of Job. Job chapter 32 says this, "I thought, 'Age should speak; advanced years should teach wisdom.' But it is the spirit in a person, the breath of the Almighty, that gives them understanding."[2]

I don't mention this because of how old you are; that's irrelevant. I mention this because of what the Lord said to me when I read over this verse, and this is what I heard, "Mike, if you want Me, come and get Me." This was a landmark experience for me. This was a simple little phrase that changed everything. It was almost as if God Himself was saying, "Mike, there is nothing or no one that will stop Me from giving Myself to you if you want Me." "Mike, I am ready and willing to continue to be found by you if you would make the decision to come and find Me." "Mike, I am willing

---

[2] Job 32:7-8, NIV

to invest Myself into anyone that is willing to invest themselves into Me." That day I made a decision, a decision to go after God with everything I had…and I have not looked back.

In Matthew chapter 25 there is a story that has been labeled The Parable of the Talents.[3] In this story a master calls his servants to himself before traveling to a far country and invests his goods to them. One receives five talents, one receives two, and another one talent. At the end of the description of how many talents were given to each of the servants there is a peculiar little phrase. The Bible says, "to each according to his ability…."[4] The master was intentional about what he decided to give to all of the servants that he called to himself.

Consider with me for a moment that the master was the one who decided to call his servants to himself and to make an intentional investment into their life. This was not something that they asked for. It was the call of the master that put them into the position to receive the investment. The master gave to each one according to their ability; there was an evaluation that had been completed before the servants were called, for the master had been watching.

Once called, it was not about being better than the one they were standing next to. Their investment

---

[3] Matt. 25:14-30, NKJV
[4] Matt. 25:14-15, NKJV

had already been determined. Once called, it was not time to begin explaining why the investment should be more than what was being given. Once called, there was only one thing needed, and that was to now go out and steward well what was given and cause the greatest return on that investment possible.

The story does not conclude with the investment. A few verses later reveal to us that the master comes back looking for a return on his investment. Really? Yes. The master was not just making random investments. There was a return that was expected, and this is what he came back looking for.

Have you ever stopped to think about the enormity of the investment that God has made into your life?

I will say it again because it is worth repeating, we have one shot at this thing called life. Have you ever stopped to think about the enormity of the investment that God has made into your life? What more could God possibly give you that could be greater than His person, the Holy Spirit? We have been given a God-sized investment, and this investment is not being given without expectation. In fact, there is a great expectation that has been laid upon the life of a man or woman filled with God. What is it that God could possibly expect from someone who is filled with Him? God expects you to change the world.

One day the Master, Jesus, will return, and He will be looking for a return on His investment. What is it that you will decide to invest your life into? What choices will you make day to day that will, at the end of your days, produce an offering to God? What return is it that you will have to offer back to the Master?

Today you can decide to allow God to do something in your heart and life far greater than anything you could ever manage or maintain in your own strength.

Today is the day of decision. Today is the day that you can make one of the most important decisions of your life. Today you can decide to let God mess up all of your plans. Today you can decide to allow God to do something in your heart and life far greater than anything you could ever manage or maintain in your own strength. Today can be the day that you decide to finally go all in with Jesus. Today you can make the decision to push all of your chips into the center of the table. We have got one shot; what will you do with yours? The clock is ticking....

1

To Be Continued

❦

John 14:12

"I tell you the truth; anyone who has faith in me will do what I have been doing, and they will do even greater things than these, because I am going to the Father."[5]

Leonard Ravenhill is known for a quote that I feel is very appropriate as we begin our journey together. The quote is this, "Are you living for things that are worth Christ dying for?"[6] My intention is not for this statement to cause a sense of guilt or condemnation to settle upon you for the life that you are

_____

[5] John 14:12, NIV
[6] Leonard Ravenhill's Ministry Quotes, http://www.leonard-ravenhill.com/quotes.

currently living. Rather I am praying that you awaken to the intimate invitation that is before you to the life of what God has always intended for those who would

If you have ever thought there was more to this life than what you have been experiencing, you are absolutely in the right place, because there is!

follow after Jesus. There is more to God than what we have been willing to be satisfied with. Bill Johnson says it best, and that is, "God will only entrust to you as much of Himself as you are willing to jealously guard."[7] We must first realize that our current experience is not all that there is to God, and then become passionate for the abundant life that Jesus said He came to give.[8]

Have you ever woken up and asked yourself, "Is this really all that there is to this life?" I have. There has to be more to life than just attempting to fill our schedules with the right religious activities. There has to be more to following Jesus than just making sure that I can keep my church attendance in good standing, or filling the offering plate with the right percentages on a monthly basis. If you have ever thought there

---

[7] "Hosting His Presence," Bill Johnson, http://bjm.org/hosting-his-presence/.
[8] John 10:10, NIV

was more to this life than what you have been experiencing, you are absolutely in the right place, because there is! There is so much more that has been made available to us.

The enemy of our souls is not afraid of your attending a church. Your surrounding yourself with the right friends and relationships does not intimidate him. He's not so much concerned if whether or not you have all of the most current worship tracks memorized. However, I will tell you what terrifies him and causes him to throw things at you to where you never come to this place. He is absolutely terrified to think that: One day you will completely yield your life to God, begin to be conformed to the image of the Son, and live like Jesus!

To consider what this life is supposed to look like, I don't think there is a better place or person that we can look to other than Jesus. Our life as a follower of Jesus is not to be patterned after any other person other than Jesus and Jesus alone. Jesus is our model. Jesus is the blueprint. Jesus is the patterned Son. If Jesus truly is our model for life, I think it would be imperative for us as disciples to closely examine and implement the way He lived as He walked the earth amongst men.

I would like to make a statement that we can unpack together: Jesus did not just come *for* us, but *as* us as well. This has great implications for the way that you live your life on a day-to-day basis. This statement has the potential to be a game changer for you. This statement, when understood, leaves me in a place where I can't help but be radically changed for the rest of my days—not because I will go out and do something, but because God has already done something. God has done something that now allows me to become something.

Our life as a follower of Jesus is not to be patterned after any other person other than Jesus and Jesus alone.

When we come to believe and are saved, we are for the most part extremely comfortable living in the reality that Jesus Christ, the Son of God, came in the flesh and offered Himself on the cross for the penalty and payment of my sins. It is in this that we believe that He came; He died, and resurrected, meaning God raised Him from the dead, and He is now seated at the right hand of the Father in the heavens. The book of Romans tells us that if we confess with our mouth "Jesus is Lord" and believe in our heart that God raised Him from the dead, we shall be saved.[9] We would agree together that Jesus came for us at a time when we could not do anything

---

[9] Rom. 10:9, NIV

for ourselves. At a time when we were yet still afar off, Jesus came and laid down His life for us.[10] To all of this I would expect that you could say, *Amen!*

Jesus coming for us is something that believers agree upon. However, what do I mean when I say that Christ did not just come *for us* but *as us* as well? This is what I mean. Jesus came and lived a life in front of us, as a man, that was a perfect demonstration of what God the Father had always intended for His sons and daughters to look like as they walked the earth. The immediate response is to quickly say something along the lines of this, "Well, that can't be all the way true because Jesus was not just a man; He was fully God as well." I understand where you are coming from and what you mean when you say this. Jesus was fully man and fully God at the same time. Jesus was fully a man that was fully dependent on His Father and filled fully with the Spirit of God.

The book of John chapter 3 says, "For he is sent by God. He speaks God's words, for God gives him the Spirit without limit."[11] The book of Colossians tells us, "For God in all His fullness was pleased to live in Christ."[12] The issue is not whether or not Jesus was fully man and fully God; the issue is that Jesus was a man that

---

[10] Rom. 5:8, NIV

[11] John 3:34, NLT

[12] Col. 1:19, NLT

was fully dependent on God, and so God was pleased to have His fullness live in Christ. Jesus was a man that was filled with the Spirit and fully yielded to God. Jesus was a man on whom the Dove could find a place to land and remain. Jesus was and is the perfect model of what life is to look like in the earth for men and women filled with the Spirit and yielded to God.

> **Jesus was and is the perfect model of what life is to look like in the earth for men and women filled with the Spirit and yielded to God.**

Jesus came and lived the abundant life that He promised He came to give. Jesus was not trying to offer something that He Himself didn't first demonstrate. It is ludicrous to consider that you would offer something to someone that you did not first possess; you can't give out of what you don't have. Jesus lived His life in front of men and showed them everything that the Father had made available to them that believed, and would believe.

The book of Philippians says that Jesus would not even consider equality with God something to be grasped, but that He emptied Himself and came in the form of a bondservant, and being made in the likeness of men.[13] He did not come and strut around as a god;

---

[13] Phil. 2:6-7, NASB

He came as a man, a very real human man that had to be dependent on His Father and the working of the Holy Spirit in His life. If He would have come and considered equality with God something to be grasped, He would have put Himself out of reach, but He did not. In fact, He's very reachable. Jesus came through the womb of a virgin and wrapped Himself in the flesh of humanity in order that He might influence the world we live in. Jesus emptied Himself of all of His advantages, made Himself vulnerable, and walked the walk. This changes everything.

Jesus emptied Himself of all of His advantages, made Himself vulnerable, and walked the walk. This changes everything.

Jesus came, demonstrated what God had always intended, and then told the disciples something very astonishing after He resurrected, yet before He ascended. He said this, "But I tell you the truth, it is to your advantage that I go away; for if I do not go away, the Helper will not come to you; but if I go, I will send Him to you."[14] Jesus was telling the disciples that it was a greater benefit for Him to go away, to ascend into the heavens, because then He would send the Helper to them, the Holy Spirit.

---

[14] John 16:7, NASB

The time had come for Jesus to not just be about His Father's business in front of them, but now He would ascend to the heavens, send the Holy Spirit, and fill the disciples with Himself, that He might continue to be about the Father's business in them and through them! Jesus is no longer standing beside men, but inside men, that He might partner with men and women in the earth that are yielded to God and full of the Holy Spirit.

We must come to the place where we stop making excuses for our lack of experience. We cannot justify our lacks in life and make doctrines out of them because we are unwilling to fully invest ourselves and pursue all that has been made available to us. It is hard to do something that you have never seen done, but once you have seen it, it becomes accessible. Jesus did not leave the disciples with any excuses. He said, "Come and follow Me and watch as I demonstrate in front of you, for you to see and be a witness, to see what life could be like for you!" Jesus demonstrated what life is like for a man or woman genuinely and intimately connected to God in

Jesus is no longer standing beside men, but inside men, that He might partner with men and women in the earth that are yielded to God and full of the Holy Spirit.

the earth, fulfilling the heart of the Father. Now we must go and do the same.

The disciples, who were still not getting all that Jesus was saying and doing, even though they had the privilege of Jesus living life in front of them, asked Him a question in John 14. They said, "Lord, show us the Father and that will be enough for us."[15] Jesus' response is one that I want to write out in its full length because of the enormous importance that it has for what we are currently examining:

> Jesus answered: "Don't you know me, Phillip, even after I have been among you such a long time? Anyone who has seen me has seen the Father. How can you say, 'Show us the Father'? Don't you believe that I am in the Father, and that the Father is in me? The words I say to you are not just my own. Rather, it is the Father, living in me, who is doing his work. Believe me when I say that I am in the Father and the Father is in me; or at least believe on the evidence of the miracles themselves. I tell you the truth; anyone who has faith in me will do what I have been doing. He will do even greater things than these, because I am going

---

[15] John 14:8, NIV

to the Father. And I will do whatever you ask in my name, so that the Son may bring glory to the Father. You may ask me anything in my name, and I will do it.[16]

Let's look at a few key things together that Jesus is telling Phillip as He responds to him in these verses. The first thing is that Jesus says, "The Father is in me."

We need to come to the place where we truly believe with all of our hearts...that the fullness of God has been invested into us in the person of the Holy Spirit.

We need to come to the place where we truly believe with all of our hearts, because the Bible says that it is with our heart that we believe,[17] that the fullness of God has been invested into us in the person of the Holy Spirit. Theologically we would amen this statement. But I am not asking you to embrace some head knowledge that, up until this point in your life, has not produced any genuine change in your daily experience and expression. I am asking you to take a moment and consider, in what way would your life be dramatically different if you really believed that the fullness of God has been invested into you? You can,

---

[16] John 14:9-14, NIV
[17] Rom. 10:9, NIV

and should, stand in great confidence to say the very words that Jesus spoke to Phillip on that day: "The Father is in me!"

Many times our challenge with this is not that we don't believe God is who He says He is. We believe that God is awesome, and glorious, and all-powerful. We believe that God can do all things. We know that God is amazing, but for some reason it becomes a challenge to really believe that same God is alive in me

Don't allow unbelief to keep you captive to a life that is less than what Jesus died and rose for you to have.

through the power and person of the Holy Spirit. The fact is this, if I really believed that the fullness of God has been invested into my life, nobody would have to tell me to step out and be different. It would be an automatic byproduct of a truth that has rocked my heart and changed the reality of my life. Jesus says to Phillip, "Don't you believe that I am in the Father and that the Father is in me?"[18] The issue here is one of doubt and unbelief.

Don't allow doubt and unbelief to rob you of the life that Jesus promised was made available to you. Don't allow unbelief to keep you captive to a life

---

[18] John 14:10, NIV

that is less than what Jesus died and rose for you to have. Just as Jesus knew that the Father was in Him, we too should have a confidence that the Father is in us. He is in you. He is in you and He wants out. Don't keep the Holy Spirit hostage in your life by your unbelief.

Second, Jesus says that it is the Father in Him that is doing His works. This is an incredible thought to meditate on: *Jesus was dependent upon the Holy Spirit to work in His life.* Jesus did not come and flex His muscles of deity; He emptied himself, became dependent upon His Father, and let God work in and through Him by the Holy Spirit. How mind blowing is it to consider that Jesus, although being the Son of God, did not just come and strut around doing His own thing for the time that He was among us in flesh? He modeled what surrender to God truly looks like. He fully surrendered Himself to God, and because of that, God was delighted to put the fullness of who He is in Him.[19]

Lastly, Jesus says "greater things than these will you do if you have faith in Me." This means there is something for us to do, and not just something, but greater things, according to Jesus! What was it exactly that Jesus did? When Jesus says that there is more for

---

[19] Col. 1:19, NIV

us to do, what types of things can we believe that He is expecting us to go forward and do?

We could develop a very long and extensive list that would include: preaching and teaching about the Kingdom of God, healing the sick, casting out demons, raising the dead, and performing signs, wonders, and miracles. Our list could also include: loving the seemingly unlovable, obedience to the Father even at the cost of our life, and forgiveness for our enemies. If we were to develop a list, we could also add to it: investing ourselves into others that

> **You are a walking God encounter. You are the way the Father has chosen to reveal Himself, or make Himself known, in the earth.**

will lead and continue running with the vision, and many other things.

Regardless of how exhaustive of a list you would want to create, I believe there is something that Jesus did that would have to find a place at the top of the list as far as expectations of what our life is to look like in the earth, and that is this: Jesus revealed the Father to those He encountered. John chapter 1 tells us that, "No one has ever seen God. The One and Only Son—the One who is at the Father's side—He has revealed Him."[20]

---

[20] John 1:18, HCSB

Jesus revealed the Father in the earth. Jesus was a God encounter.

Our lives are to be God encounters in the earth. You have the wonderful privilege of revealing the Father in the earth. When people encounter you they should encounter God. You are a walking God encounter. You are the way the Father has chosen to reveal Himself, or make Himself known, in the earth.

God desires to be made known through a people the same way that His Son revealed Him as He lived among us. God is looking for a people that would allow Him to break in to their life. God is jealously on the hunt for a man or a woman that would yield their life to Him so that He can change the world. When God was ready to make history and change a generation, He put one man into the earth, Jesus, filled Him with the fullness of the Holy Spirit, and let Him loose! I am praying for a people that God can fill up and let loose into the earth!

God not only wants to get in...He is looking for someone that would let Him out!

The stage has been set. Your part has been crafted by the hands of the Father and awaits you. The book of Romans says, "For the anxious longing of the creation waits eagerly for the revealing of the sons of God."[21] All of creation is waiting for you to reveal what it is that you are carrying. What you have locked up on the inside is desperately needed on the outside. Creation is waiting. Many are comfortable letting God in...but God not only wants to get in...He is looking for someone that would let Him out!

---

[21] Rom. 8:19, NASB

Please take a few moments to watch my video
and continue to be challenged on
what it means to be a part of:

"God's Continuation!"

https://vimeo.com/122153986

2

Public vs. Personal

—∞∞∞—

2 Chronicles 16:9

"For the eyes of the Lord run to and fro throughout the whole earth, to show Himself strong on behalf of those whose heart is loyal to Him...."[22]

Matthew chapter 16 gives us a very important section of Scripture that I believe has tremendous meaning for where we find ourselves today with what God is doing in the earth. For the next couple of chapters I would like to take Matthew chapter 16, and verse-by-verse, walk through verse 13 down to verse 25. In this I believe that we will be able to

---

[22] 2 Chron. 16:9, NKJV

identify a clear progression, a plan if you would, for the way that Jesus Himself lays out for God to break into a generation!

Beginning with verse 13 the Bible tells us, "When Jesus came to the region of Caesarea Philippi, he asked his disciples, 'Who do people say the son of man is?'"[23] This may seem like a simple, straightforward question, but let's look together at what is actually happening here. Jesus comes into a region, that being the region of Caesarea Philippi, and turns to those who have been walking with Him for some time now and poses a question to them about what people are saying about Him in this specific region. This is not a coincidence. This is not just a conversation starter or small talk; Jesus is after something. There was obviously something being said about Jesus that He wanted to know...or that He wanted the disciples to know. The question is very pointed, and it comes with a purpose.

There was obviously something being said about Jesus that He wanted to know...or that He wanted the disciples to know.

Upon receiving the question the disciples are quick to answer. Verse 14 tells us, "They replied, 'Some say

---

[23] Matt. 16:13, NIV

John the Baptist; others say Elijah; and still others, Jeremiah or one of the prophets.'"[24] Now, interestingly enough, the disciples seem to answer fairly quickly, which tells me that they had to be familiar with what was being said about Jesus around town. They were up-to-date with the word on the streets about who Jesus was. The disciples had knowledge of what the public perception of Jesus was and the way that He was being portrayed through the comments of people in this specific region that they had just walked into. Jesus is looking for Intel and the disciples are able to provide just that.

Once the disciples provide Jesus with what is being said about Him in this region, He presents them with another question, and with this question we move from public to personal. Verse 15 tells us, "'But what about you?' he asked. 'Who do you say I am?'"[25] This time Jesus is not just asking if they are familiar with what it is that people have to say about Him. Now He wants to know what the disciples themselves have to say about Him. This is huge, and is again, not just a way to small talk with His team as they were traveling about.

I want to take a moment to give careful attention to what is actually happening here before we continue

---

[24] Matt. 16:14, NIV
[25] Matt. 16:15, NIV

into the next few verses. It is important that we grasp the severity of these seemingly insignificant verses. It is very easy in our reading of this portion of Scripture to breeze over these two questions and move on in the story, but I want to park here for a moment and dissect this interaction between Jesus and His chosen team that He is walking with.

These two questions that Jesus is asking here are critical for us as believers today. In fact, I would even go as far as to say that I don't believe that there are two more important questions that face us as followers of Jesus in our generation. The same two questions that Jesus offered to His disciples that day as they walked into the region of Caesarea Philippi are the same two questions that He is offering to us as disciples today, in our generation, as we walk with Him: Who do men say that I am? Who do you say that I am?

Let's rewind for just a moment to where all of this begins in Matthew chapter 16; we began with verse 13. Jesus and His disciples come walking into a new region. In this new region Jesus is interested in what people are saying about Him. The comments of people in a region have now created a public opinion, or perception, of Jesus that He wants to find out about. The disciples are able to provide Jesus with what it is that people think about Him, and are saying about Him, in the region that they are currently standing in.

In fact, the disciples say that some think Jesus is John the Baptist; others think that he is Elijah; and still others are saying that He is Jeremiah the prophet. This may seem like a strange thought process for sure for people to have, until you realize something: these were people that were familiar with the *activity of Jesus*. These were people that had for sure heard about Jesus. In fact, Jesus was the talk of the town in many places that He walked through and ministered.

Jesus was the highlight of many conversations in those days.

Whether you loved Him or hated Him, whether you agreed or disagreed, or whether you really understood what was happening before your eyes, Jesus was the highlight of many conversations in those days. These were probably people that had followed Him and been spectators in the crowd as Jesus was drawing attention in whatever place it was He was moving through and ministering in. The buzz about Jesus would have come from people that were familiar with the *activity of Jesus*.

Some said that He was John the Baptist? This makes sense when you consider that Jesus went about preaching, "Repent, for the kingdom of heaven is at hand."[26] Many would have been familiar with John's message, and his recent imprisonment and beheading

---

[26] Matt. 4:17, NASB

by King Herod.[27] Others thought that He was Elijah? This very well could have been because they saw Him perform miracles and work wonders; Elijah being the great miracle working prophet from the Old Testament in the book of 1 Kings. And still some were saying that He was Jeremiah? This would have been because they would have seen Him weep over Jerusalem because of how He longed to gather them.[28]

This perspective in the region was developed from people that knew a piece of Jesus; their vantage point left them with a fractional understanding of who He was and what He was all about. These were people that found themselves in a place where their idea of Jesus was developed off of what they saw Him doing. Again, these were people that were familiar with the *activity of Jesus.* The thing to take note of here is this: *You can be familiar with activity and not be connected to identity.* They knew what Jesus was doing...they just did not really know who He was.

For many, this is the place they find themselves. All they know is what Jesus is able to do for them. They are only familiar with the activity of Jesus, and because of this, they are stuck with a fractional view of who Jesus really is. Some have developed entire doctrinal positions off of a piece of Jesus, and though

---

[27] Matt. 14:1-2, NIV
[28] Matt. 23:27, NIV

that one piece may be true, it is not enough. There is more to Jesus than just the piece that we are comfortable with, even more than just what we have been willing to receive.

What is it that people around you have to say about Jesus? Is there a public opinion of the Son of Man that does not line up with His true identity? Any idea or thought process that we have about Jesus that is not represented in the Word of God is false and needs to be discarded. Jesus is the perfect representation of God and we cannot formulate opinions about Him that are based off of our thoughts of what we think God should be like, or our limited understanding and interpretation of what we want the Scriptures to say.

> **Jesus is the perfect representation of God and we cannot formulate opinions about Him that are based off of our thoughts of what we think God should be like.**

We cannot even come to conclusions about Jesus based on our lack of experience. What do I mean? What I mean is this: you cannot determine that Jesus is not the healer just because you have not personally been healed, or seen anyone healed. Jesus is much greater than our opinion of Him, and in fact, He is not bound or limited to your opinion about Him.

At times, and maybe this is true for where you live, there is a Jesus that is talked about and preached about in public, or at large, that does not line up with who Jesus really is. Maybe characteristics are added to Jesus. Possibly characteristics are subtracted from Jesus. It is quite possible with the methods of addition and subtraction for the culture to create a Jesus that does not even really exist.

Jesus is much greater than our opinion of Him, and in fact, He is not bound or limited to your opinion about Him.

Why would I say such a thing? Many times people want a Jesus that would say what they would say, or do what they would do, in a given situation. People desire a God that is more like us, and more formed to our image than we are to His so that they can justify the thoughts they have or the behaviors they are unwilling to part with. For many it comes down to it being as simple as this: I am unwilling to change.

If I am unwilling to change, then that means Jesus must change, or not be who you say He is, in order for me to be willing to accept Him. Many have created a Jesus to their liking, and are supposedly walking with and worshiping a Jesus that does not really exist. And in the midst of all this commotion and confusion swirling around about the identity of Jesus, the question still remains: Who do people say the Son of Man is? As the disciples were on that day, we too must be able to discern what the crowd is saying about Jesus.

Next, Jesus moves from public to personal with the disciples. Now, Jesus is not just looking for what the crowd is saying about Him; He wants to know what those who have been walking with Him and doing life with Him have to say about Him. You see, there is a greater accountability that rests upon the lives of those who actually claim to walk with Jesus, and Jesus will not just continue on and allow the answer to this question to be bypassed. The question to the disciples is now: "What do you say about Me?"

What do you say about Jesus? Who do you say that he is? A. W. Tozer said it best when he said, "What comes into our minds when we think about God is the most important thing about us."[29] As a follower of Jesus, you must be able to differentiate between what the crowd is saying about Jesus and what you are saying about Jesus. These answers will not always be the same.

Let's say we, in a present-day context, are disciples of Jesus, and are traveling with Him into a certain region. How do you answer this question? What is it that you have to say when God turns to you

---

[29] "A. W. Tozer Quotes," Good Reads, http://www.goodreads.com/author/quotes/1082290.A_W_Tozer.

face-to-face, and asks you for your definition of who He is to you? I can only imagine the hesitation that must have set in for the disciples as they scrambled within themselves to come up with a worthy enough response to Jesus' question. I can imagine that some of them would have turned aside as if something or someone was catching their attention. I can see some of them attempting to look away in order to avoid eye contact with Jesus, hoping that another would offer a response before one was required from them. It would be no different for most of us today if we were faced with the same scenario. Yet, however we attempt to dodge this question, Jesus lovingly, patiently stands, and He waits. He waits because He must know what is in your heart before He moves on. This question is not an end to itself; it is actually a beginning…and the question remains: *Who do you say that I am?*

Time of Testing

At this point in our time together I have to insert, or bring to light, if you would, a truth that you must be aware of. Do not just downplay these two questions that Jesus is asking His disciples. Do not write them off and think that they don't hold any value in your life with anything that you are facing or going through. You may be thinking to yourself, "Do you have any idea all that I have going on right now? I don't have time to sit and think about how I would respond to these questions." Fair enough. Let's take a deeper look at this.

You may not have time to sit down and intentionally give thought to your answers to these questions. But one thing I know to be true is this: You are already answering these questions by the way you are living your life. You are answering these questions by the way you are responding to life and the scenarios that are unfolding in front of you. You are answering these questions, whether or not it is verbal, by your behavior. I have always said that I don't need to have a man tell me what he believes; just let me see the way he behaves long enough and I will tell you what he believes. Behavior will always give evidence to what is really believed in the heart.

Behavior will always give evidence to what is really believed in the heart.

Could it be that every test in your life is an attempt to get you to shift your answer to one of these two questions? I believe so. You have to mature from the place where you simply believe that the enemy is continually forming weapons against you because he is after your stuff. The enemy is not simply after your stuff. This fight is not one that is being waged for the temporal situations in your life. This fight is being fought, not for your situation, but for your revelation. The enemy is after who you say that Jesus is.

Think about it...every trial, every fight, every weapon that has been put together with strategic intention against you, because that is what Isaiah tells us in chapter 54[30], is not simply just trying to cause you to be broke, lose friends, ruin your business, or have you to be sick all the time. That would be easy enough to accomplish if that were all that the enemy was after. We must realize that the enemy cares more about my revelation than my situation. The enemy wants to use my situation to deteriorate, or cause me to willingly surrender, my revelation. If this is the case, and if this is where the battle lines are being drawn, then my answer to, "Who do I say the Son of Man is?" becomes very important. It actually becomes my lifeline in times when I feel I am drowning under the pressures and trials of life. I have written more about this subject specifically in another place, *Free Indeed,*[31] so I will not belabor the point here.

The fight you are currently facing that may involve your finances is not just about your money; it is about the revelation of Jesus in your life that says He is the

---

[30] Isa 54:17, NASB

[31] Michael Dow, *Free Indeed* (Burning Ones, 2013) Available at amazon. com, http://www.amazon.com/Free-Indeed-Life-Obedience/dp/ 0989218503.

provider. It is a fight to maintain your belief in the reality that, "My God will supply all my needs according to His riches in glory in Christ Jesus."[32] Your fight for the health of your body, though it may include doctors' reports and the opinions of those who are considered to be practicing professionals, is really about the revelation of Jesus in your life that says He is the healer. It is a fight to maintain your belief that says, "by His wounds I have been healed."[33] This application can be made for any revelation that you have received, or are found to be true in the Word of God, about Jesus in your life.

> **Your fight for the health of your body...is really about the revelation of Jesus in your life that says He is the healer.**

Can you see it? The enemy would love nothing more than to see you deny the Son of Man and willingly surrender your revelation because of the external pressure that is being applied in your life. The enemy would love to see you turn your back on your answer to who Jesus is during an intense struggle. At times you will have to look right into the face of a situation that seems to be in direct contradiction to who God says He is in your life and say to yourself, "Despite

---

[32] Phil. 4:19, NASB

[33] 1 Peter 2:24, NIV

what I see with my eyes, I will not deny what He has shown me in my heart!" For the Bible tells us that it is with the heart that you truly believe.[34]

God-Consciousness

Let's, for just a moment, take a look at the life of Job and how his story illustrates the point that we are driving home here beautifully. If you remember, Job really went through it. Yet it was not unfaithfulness, or disobedience, that brought about the storms and trials in Job's life. Actually it was quite the opposite; the enemy came after Job because of God's testimony about Job. It was said of Job, by God, that there was no one on the earth like him, a blameless and upright man who fears God and turns away from evil.[35] There are worse things that could be said about you. Job seems to be doing pretty good for himself, and God obviously was very aware of the way Job had committed himself to live.

The thing that I want you to notice about Job's story is this: The enemy could not take Job's revelation, or God-consciousness. The enemy could touch all that Job had, and seem to remove certain things from his life. Yet, even with all that the enemy could

---

[34] Rom. 10:9, NASB
[35] Job 1:8, NASB

touch and take away, there was one thing that Job would have had to forfeit in order for the enemy to gain control of it and that is this: his revelation of who God was to him! Sure, the enemy was able to touch his family, his finances, and even Job's health. But even with all of what he was able to touch, the only way that the enemy could have changed Job's mind about who God was is to have Job willingly turn away from the revelation that he carried about God in his life.

> **Job had a *God-consciousness* in his life that he was willing to fight for, and would not surrender.**

Even when those closest to Job, his wife to mention specifically, attempted to get Job to turn his back on his revelation, Job would not.[36] Job had a *God-consciousness* in his life that he was willing to fight for, and would not surrender. What do I mean when I say *God-consciousness*? Simply put, I mean this: the awareness of God's presence with you.

Is it possible to be aware of God in your life? Is God's presence really something that we can sense, or know? I would shout an astounding YES! In fact, reflecting back to the garden where all of this begins, with God and Adam, the Bible tells us that God

---

[36] Job 2:9, NIV

walked in the garden amongst Adam and Eve in the cool of the day.[37] Adam and Eve knew the presence of God, or had such a strong consciousness of God, that when God came walking in the garden they hid themselves. This was not a surprise arrival by God. Adam and Eve were aware enough of the presence that they knew when God was there, and also in point, when He was not.

Now, you may think to yourself: *Okay, I hear what you are saying, but that was back in the garden of Eden, in the Old Testament, and that's not really something that we can fight for today.* And to that I would fast-forward to the New Testament to the apostle Paul who writes to the church at Corinth. In the book of 2 Corinthians chapter 10 Paul makes this statement in verse 5, "We demolish arguments and every pretension that sets itself up against the knowledge of God, and we take captive every thought to make it obedient to Christ."[38]

What does Paul mean when he says, "the knowledge of God"? I would argue that Paul is not talking about some theological head knowledge. Paul is not telling them that arguments will come against them that will attempt to undermine, or override, the mental ascent to which they have agreed upon the existence of God. Sure that may be a small piece of what Paul

---

[37] Gen. 3:8, NIV
[38] 2 Cor. 10:5, NIV

means, or it may be wrapped up into the point that he is getting at, but there is much more to this statement than a mere working head knowledge of God.

Paul understood something that is imperative for us as believers to connect with, and that is this: we have been given the present knowledge, or the ability to know God in the moment. In this moment you can know God. Yes, you can know God right now, and in fact God has gone to great lengths in order for you to have the opportunity to know Him in the moment.

Jesus, who is the exact representation of God in the earth,[39] told the disciples in the book of John, "But very truly I tell you, it is good for you that I am going away. Unless I go away, the Advocate will not come to you; but if I go, I will send him to you."[40] What was Jesus talking about? Jesus was describing to the disciples that up until that point they had walked with a God-consciousness because Jesus had been walking beside them. Now, upon His ascension into the heavens to the right hand of the Father, Jesus

> **You can know God right now, and in fact God has gone to great lengths in order for you to have the opportunity to know Him in the moment.**

---

[39] Heb. 1:3, NASB
[40] John 16:7, NIV

would now send them the Holy Spirit, which would be God Himself living inside them. Jesus no longer stands on the outside, but now He stands on the inside. This is something we will talk about in greater detail in a later chapter. But for now, just realize, we have been given the presence of God.

God, in the person of Jesus, has come to us and now remains with us and in us by the Holy Spirit...*always*!

After Jesus was crucified and had resurrected, He appeared to the disciples and spoke to them about the Kingdom of God.[41] In the last chapter of the book of Matthew, in what is known as the Great Commission, Jesus concludes with this statement to the disciples, "And surely I am with you always, to the very end of the age."[42] God, in the person of Jesus, has come to us and now remains with us and in us by the Holy Spirit...*always*! The very meaning of His name that Isaiah prophesied about, being Immanuel,[43] means: God with us. This word that Jesus used, always, is something that I would like to expound upon because I believe this is what Paul was echoing

---

[41] Acts 1:3, NASB

[42] Matt. 28:20, NIV

[43] Isa. 7:14, NASB

when he encouraged the church at Corinth to fight for *God-consciousness.*

Let's return to Paul's statement, "And we demolish arguments and every pretension that sets itself up against the knowledge of God...."[44] Here Paul says that they are to demolish arguments that set themselves up against the knowledge of God. Well, what is an argument? An argument is defined as this: an exchange of diverging or opposite views. To make this simple, an argument is when you have two different opinions that are being communicated against one another. If we are to maintain our *God-consciousness* we must be aware of this reality: there are opposing viewpoints that will attempt to compete with, or replace, the one we may carry.

If we are to maintain our *God-consciousness* we must be aware of this reality: there are opposing viewpoints that will attempt to compete with, or replace, the one we may carry.

What is the first thing that typically happens whenever you encounter trial, tribulation, or weapons that have been formed against you? This may not be a blanket application for all, but I have heard from

---

[44] 2 Cor. 10:5, NIV

many that the first thought that usually scrolls through their mind is something like this: *Where is God in all of this?* Or how about this one: *If God were really with me, how could this happen?* We need to be very aware in the moment whenever we begin to walk into the situations of life that may be intense, damaging, or working against us in whatever fashion that there are competing arguments attempting to cause us to surrender our *God-consciousness.*

Maybe this just applies to me, but I know that I have been through seasons of life where it seemed as if I was more aware of my emotions than I was the presence of God. I have been through trials where I was more problem-conscious than I was God-conscious; more bill-conscious than God-conscious. I have been through some very intense struggles that have caused me to be more self-conscious, or aware of my surroundings and those things pressing in up against me than I was God-conscious for sure.

It is during these times that your situations of life would want you to believe: God has left you, which is why you are going through what you are going through. I know there are certain viewpoints out there that want you to believe that God will leave you for "dark seasons," or however they choose to word these periods in your walk where God will move away from you or become very distant in order to serve some greater purpose…I could not disagree with this type of thinking more. I can't think this way whenever I continually hear the words of Jesus resounding in my heart that say, "I am with you *always*!"

Again, God has gone to great lengths in order to give Himself to us. Whenever we are going through the fiery trials of life we need to fight for God-consciousness. Opposing thoughts, competing arguments, and the whispers of the enemy may come…but regardless of what may be presented to you in the moment, no matter how contradictory your scenario may be to what God has said, God is with you and has committed Himself to you until the end of the age. At any moment we can choose to retreat from the tension on the outside, and inwardly we can set our gaze upon Jesus, and in that place, regardless of what is happening around us, we can find rest. We can continually walk with God-consciousness when we fight to break through the other awarenesses that attempt to rob us of it.

Opposing thoughts, competing arguments, and the whispers of the enemy may come… but God is with you and has committed Himself to you until the end of the age.

This is something that definitely does not just fall into your lap. It is not something that is just going to be an easy walk through the park. This is a fight. This fight is very intense. This is something that you will have to determine to train yourself in. Once you commit yourself in this direction you can rest assured that there would be plenty of opportunities for you to prove this point. However, whatever we must do, we must, in order to remain more aware of God's presence in our life than any other thing. You can be certain of this: the devil would love nothing more than for you to remain more self-conscious than you are God-conscious. You must fight for God-consciousness!

Please take a few moments to watch this stirring
video from one of today's most prominent
and powerful voices.

"Who Is Jesus to You?"

https://vimeo.com/122154138

3

Prioritizing Pursuits

———⊗⊗⊗———

Hebrews 11:6

> "And without faith it is impossible to please
> Him, for he who comes to God must believe
> that He is and that He is the rewarder of those
> who seek Him."[45]

Let's return to our story that is unfolding in
Matthew chapter 16. Jesus and His traveling
ministry team have entered into a region and Jesus
has put to the disciples two amazing questions that
we've already explored. It is at this point that Peter
steps up and has an answer for Jesus. In fact, he has
the profound revelation, in verse 16, "You are the

---

[45] Heb. 11:6, NASB

Christ, the Son of the living God."[46] Wow! This is not just a good answer; this is something that Jesus actually applauds and responds to in verse 17 by saying, "Blessed are you, Simon Barjona, because flesh and blood did not reveal this to you, but my Father who is in heaven. I also say to you that you are Peter, and upon this rock I will build my church; and the gates of Hades will not overpower it."[47]

Jesus tells Peter that flesh and blood did not reveal to him the understanding of who He was that he had in that moment, but that his Father gave him revelation; this is amazing. Taking Jesus' response we can pull out two simple things that He is letting us in on by what it is He is saying to Peter in that moment, and that is this: there are revelations that can come from flesh and blood, and then there are revelations that only the Father can give. This is a very simple, yet weighty truth when we understand its application.

I am jealous for a revelation of Jesus that comes from the Father. I am jealous for the Father to give you a revelation of Jesus. The Father reveals Jesus to us by the working and the power of the Holy Spirit. It is one of the many roles of the Holy Spirit to reveal Jesus to us, to make Jesus very real to us. We absolutely need the Holy Spirit.

---

[46] Matt. 16:16, NASB
[47] Matt. 16:17-18, NASB

The revelation of Jesus that the Holy Spirit installs into our life is not just a one-time event. It is not like we catch a glimpse of Jesus one day and then we are good for the rest of our life; at least that is not how it is supposed to work. The Holy Spirit continually, day by day, moment by moment, wants to make Jesus real to us. The Holy Spirit lovingly and joyfully unveils the beauty of the Son to those who believe. I don't know where I would be without the working of the Holy Spirit in my life to relentlessly work with me to have my eyes opened to the reality of Jesus.

The Holy Spirit continually, day by day, moment by moment, wants to make Jesus real to us. The Holy Spirit lovingly and joyfully unveils the beauty of the Son to those who believe.

Why is it so important that we press in, and push forward, for a revelation of Jesus that comes from the Father by the Spirit? It is very easy to just settle for what Jesus describes as *flesh and blood revealing that to you*. This language that Jesus uses speaks to me and lets me know that it is possible for a revelation, as great as it may be, to be passed on from one person to the next, flesh and blood revealing something to me. I am not against learning about who Jesus is from those around us; that is absolutely not what I am saying whatsoever. However, with that being said, I am against people not having an encounter for themselves and simply being satisfied with listening to other people about a Jesus that they do not yet know, or have not yet seen, for themselves.

When all you do is trust in people to reveal Jesus to you, without going to the Father and asking Him to make Jesus real to you by the power of the Holy Spirit, your revelation of Jesus, again regardless of how great it may be, will be limited to the experience of the man or woman that you are using as a lifeline to Jesus in your life. You will never be able to outgrow the revelation of the one in whom you have placed your eyes upon to talk to you about Jesus. A person will never be able to lead you to a revelation of Jesus that they themselves have not had. The cap on your revelation will be the person in front of you, the flesh and blood that has been revealing Jesus to you.

The Holy Spirit has an eternal perspective of the Son, and this is what He comes to install into the lives of those who come to Him.

This is why we need the Holy Spirit! We need to rely upon the Holy Spirit, and be intentional about trusting the Holy Spirit, to reveal Jesus to us. The Holy Spirit has a different vantage point than we do;

the Holy Spirit sees Jesus in a much different way than we do. The Holy Spirit has an eternal perspective of the Son, and this is what He comes to install into the lives of those who come to Him. The Holy Spirit in you is constantly working to work out the revelation of Jesus to you.

Jesus is an endless revelation, and when we trust the Holy Spirit to reveal Jesus to us, our journey of knowing Jesus becomes endless. Once this life as we know it comes to an end and we enter into what it is that God has in store for all who believe, we will for all of eternity behold the glory of the Lamb, the precious Son who was slain before the foundations of the world. We will never have Jesus all figured out. We will literally, for all of eternity, continue to be in awe of the revelation of Jesus. Praise God!

Jesus is an endless revelation, and when we trust the Holy Spirit to reveal Jesus to us, our journey of knowing Jesus becomes endless.

If we will forever be in awe of Jesus, then woe be it unto us who feel as if we have become satisfied with however much of Jesus we feel has already been revealed to us. Jesus is an endless ocean of revelation, and to those who are willing to plunge out into the depths, He will never leave you to drown unsatisfied.

I pray that even as you are reading over these words that something on the inside of you will begin to stir. I pray that hunger awakens on the inside for the reality of Jesus in your life.

Hebrews says that he that comes to God…He is the rewarder of those.[48] Hear me, it does not say that He is the rewarder of those that casually sit by on the sidelines satisfied and full. It says that to those that are hungry enough to come, He is faithful enough to feed. God is faithful to feed the hungry.

Given, Not Earned

What is it that causes a man to *come to God?* Hebrews says that he that *comes to God* must believe that He is…I would argue that we cannot come to God on our own. Jesus said that no man could come to the Father except that the Father draws him.[49] The only reason that you can come to God is because God has first come to you. The only reason that your heart can burn for God is because His heart was first burning for you.

God installs hunger into the life of a man by stirring up the Holy Spirit in him. It is this stirring that causes us to become awakened to an intense sense of

---

[48] Heb. 11:6, NIV
[49] John 6:44, NIV

longing for the presence and the person of Jesus. When we are given this opportunity, because it is an opportunity, it is not a guarantee, because it demands a response; we are at a very important place. At the time that we feel the stirring of the Holy Spirit within us we have a very crucial window of opportunity, a crossroad if you would, to make a decision. We must make a decision. This decision could possibly lead to some of the greatest breakthroughs, or break-ins, that we have ever experienced.

The only reason that your heart can burn for God is because His heart was first burning for you.

We can decide to give ourselves to the stirring and begin to step into the obedience of whatever it would mean for us, practically, to begin to come to God. Or, we can choose to ignore the stirring, which always brings us to the hardening of our heart. The continual choice to neglect the stirring of the Holy Spirit is in essence, a refusal to open the door when God is coming to you. Picture this: God is coming to you, knocking on the door of your heart...and you will not open up to let Him in.

It is important to understand, and this will even be a truth that sets some free, that our hunger for God is not self-generated. You cannot make yourself hungry for God; hunger is given to you. Hunger is something that God installs, or awakens, in your life in times and seasons when He is ready for you to progress beyond where you currently stand. Hunger is something that is gifted to you so that God can accomplish His purpose in you. Stop and consider that last statement for a moment.

Hunger is something that God installs, or awakens, in your life in times and seasons when He is ready for you to progress beyond where you currently stand.

The hunger that you have for God is not something that you worked up yourself; your hunger was given to you. The Father will install hunger into you in order to bring you to Himself. Remember, Jesus said that no man could come unless the Father drew him.[50] Rather than allowing the pressure of this thought to stagnate you, step into the freedom that this truth provides.

There has to come a time in your life when you really begin to believe that God is enough in your life to bring you to the place that He is bringing you. The Holy Spirit in you is jealous to conform you to the image of the Son. This means that your pursuit does not even belong to you, but it belongs to God. So

---

[50] John 6:44, NIV

even in the place of pursuit no man has any room to boast. Paul said that one, who boasts, let him boast in the Lord.[51]

Again, God will gift hunger to you so that He can accomplish His purposes in you; His purpose is to make you look like Jesus. The Father is far more interested in making you into something than He is in trying to get you to do something. It is impossible for us to look like Him, Jesus, unless we continually come to Him. We will continually reflect that which we continually behold.

It is impossible for us to look like Him, Jesus, unless we continually come to Him. We will continually reflect that which we continually behold.

There is great freedom in knowing that I cannot want Jesus as much as I should. What? How could I say such a thing? For me, something that I pray regularly, and not because I think I am in really bad shape spiritually, but because I realize the truth of what we have been talking about, is this: Holy Spirit, help me to love Jesus. I need the working of the Holy Spirit in my life to help me to love Jesus the way that He deserves to be loved, the way that He desires to be loved.

---

[51] 2 Cor. 10:17, NASB

At times my heart wanders. At times my thoughts are not aligned. At times I just don't want to do things I know I should do in order to keep myself in His love.[52] I am not talking about intentional sin; I am talking about things that will help to keep me "in love" with Jesus. Side note: There is a huge difference between love, and being *in love*. I can say that I love you, but there is a much different implication when I say that I am in love with you. Some of us have gotten so programmed in the way that we believe that we love Jesus that we have totally fallen out of love with Jesus and don't even realize it.

All of what we plan is great, but without the Holy Spirit revealing the Son and bringing us to the place of encounter, it is all in vain.

Isn't it time that you fell back in love with Jesus? That can't happen without you realizing that as good as your efforts are, they just won't get the job done. It is not your routine that produces love. It is not your devotional life that produces love. It is an encounter with the Son; it is actually touching the person of Jesus that causes us to fall in love. All of what we plan is great, but without the Holy Spirit revealing

---

[52] John 15:9, NIV

the Son and bringing us to the place of encounter, it is all in vain. It would be foolish for me to tell you that I love something that I have never experienced or tasted for myself.

For some, it is time to break away from the system of things that we love so much and fall back fresh in love with Jesus. For some, it is time to realize that our strength, our intellect, our discipline, is not what gets the job done, but it is an absolute relentless dependency upon the Holy Spirit to continually reveal Jesus to me...and then all of these other things fall into their right working place. For others, it is time to admit that you just don't want Him as much as your conversations that you have with others attempt to reveal you do, and that's okay, because right now you have the opportunity to open the door of your heart to the knocking of the Holy Spirit! Right now you have the wonderful invitation to come to Jesus! I pray that you would stop everything and answer right now!

Knowing Him, Knowing Me

Jesus says to Simon, "I also say to you that you are Peter...."[53] This is so powerful! Not only does Simon come into an amazing revelation of Jesus that is given to him by the Father in heaven, but also

---

[53] Matt. 16:18, NASB

Jesus reveals to him a revelation of himself that he had not yet known. This is where we learn another incredible truth: There are revelations about us that are locked up in the revelation of Jesus! There are things that we will not be able to know about ourselves until we know certain things about Him. There are revelations about you that are unlocked by stepping into greater revelations of Him! Praise God!

There are revelations about us that are locked up in the revelation of Jesus! There are things that we will not be able to know about ourselves until we know certain things about Him.

As I have written in great detail in another place, *Free Indeed,*[54] I cannot see myself completely until I see Him, Jesus, correctly. To truly know God is to truly know myself. My definition comes from God. I want to encourage you in this: You are who God says you are. You are not defined by the opinions of others. You are not simply a byproduct of your situations or limitations. You belong to God and He is the only one that has the right to define you.

In Matthew chapter 3 we find a beautiful occasion. Jesus has come to John the Baptist and is about to be

---

[54] Dow, Michael. *Free Indeed.*

baptized. After John agrees to go through with this and baptize Jesus, something very impactful happens. As Jesus is coming up out of the waters, the Bible says, "After being baptized, Jesus came up immediately from the water; and behold, the heavens were opened, and he saw the Spirit of God descending as a dove and lighting on Him, and behold, a voice out of the heavens said, 'This is My beloved Son, in whom I am well-pleased.'"[55] This is amazing!

Of all that we could talk about pertaining to this passage, I just want to simply take a look at the fact that Jesus received His definition from the voice of the Father that came out of the heavens. In front of all that were there, a voice out of the heavens declared to Jesus, and everyone else, "This is My Son, in whom I am well pleased." There was no gray area as to who Jesus was or the pleasure that His Father had about Him. It was very clear; "This is My Son, and I am pleased about that."

It is important to note here that Jesus' definition did not come from His performance. The pleasure of the Father was spoken over Jesus before His "ministry" actually began. This means that He was defined as a son before He preached His first message. The Father spoke His great pleasure over Jesus before

---

[55] Matt. 3:16-17, NASB

He worked His first miracle or drew His first crowd. Jesus was who His Father said He was; nothing more, nothing less.

You are who God says you are; nothing more, nothing less. The Father's pleasure over you and to you is not dependent upon your activity in life. Your activity does not determine your identity; the voice out of the heavens does. We must know what it is that God is saying about us. If we do not get into our Bible and find out for ourselves what it is that the Father has said about us, and who it is that we are, we will continually allow our lives to be shaped by other voices.

> **If we do not get into our Bible and find out for ourselves what it is that the Father has said about us, and who it is that we are, we will continually allow our lives to be shaped by other voices.**

There will be times and seasons when you will need to be reminded of who it is that God says you are. There will be times of struggle that will cause you to doubt. There will be times when you do not have the support of the cheerleaders on the sideline. There will be moments when the outcomes you are experiencing will attempt to persuade you that you are something other than who and what the Father has said you are. What do you do when these times come upon you? I think we find the answer for this later on in the life of Jesus in John's gospel.

There is a story in John chapter 10 that we can draw great encouragement from. Verse 40 of chapter 10 tells us, "Then Jesus went back across the Jordan to the place where John had been baptizing in the early days. There he stayed...."[56] Now, your immediate reaction may be to say, "What does this matter? How does this fit into the talk that we have been having about needing to be fully invested into believing that I am who God says I am?" I am glad you asked; let me tell you.

In order to understand the significance of this one statement that John is making to us, we must first look back at what is happening that leads into verse 40. Verses 22 through 39, in my Bible, are subheaded this way: Further Conflict Over Jesus' Claims. When you read through those verses you will find that the conflict that this subheading speaks of was the fact that Jesus was claiming to be the Son of God and the Jews did not like it.

In verse 24 of John chapter 10 the Jews ask Him outright, "How long will you keep us in suspense? If you are the Messiah, tell us plainly."[57] Jesus offers a powerful response by saying, "I did tell you, but you

---

[56] John 10:40, NIV
[57] John 10:24, NIV

do not believe. The works I do in my Father's name testify about me, but you do not believe because you are not my sheep. My sheep listen to my voice; I know them, and they follow me. I give them eternal life, and they shall never perish; no one will snatch them out of my hand. My Father, who has given them to me, is greater than all; no one can snatch them out of my Father's hand. I and the Father are one."[58]

Now, you would think that to a response like this the issue would have been settled. However, rather than believing, the Bible says that again His Jewish opponents picked up stones to stone Him.[59] What? They asked Him to finally tell them plainly and provide for them an honest answer, and when Jesus does that, they are quick to, again notice, pick up stones to stone Him for what He tells them.

Jesus then asks for which of the good works from the Father that He has done is He being stoned for, to which they reply, "We are not stoning you for any good work, but for blasphemy, because you, a mere man, claim to be God."[60] At this point Jesus provides one last effort to have their eyes opened to the reality of what He is saying and who He is, and even at this, in verse 39, it says, "Again they tried to seize him,

---

[58] John 10:25-30, NIV
[59] John 10:31, NIV
[60] John 10:32-33, NIV

but he escaped their grasp."[61] It is after all of this exchange that we come into verse 40 where Jesus has left this place and returned to the area where John was baptizing in the earlier days. It is in this small story of conflict that we can find great strength.

Jesus withdrew to the place that John had been baptizing in the earlier days. Why would this be the place that Jesus would choose to go? Was it because it was the nearest safe place He could think of? Was it because there was nowhere else for Him to go? I don't believe either of those are the answer. I believe that Jesus was in fact drawn to this place, especially after all the conflict He had just gone through with those that He was sent for. Jesus withdrew to the place John had been baptizing for a very significant reason: This is where He received definition.

Jesus withdrew to the place John had been baptizing for a very significant reason: This is where He received definition.

Jesus went to a place that would remind Him of who He really was and what He was about. Jesus went to a place that would instantly revive in Him the experience of having the voice of the Father thunder out of the heavens. Jesus went to the place where He could

---

[61] John 10:39, NIV

be reminded that He was the Son of the Father. Jesus went back to the place of encounter.

You need a place in your life that represents for you the place where John had been baptizing. You need a place that you can turn to, go to, or sit and reflect about in times when life is shouting that you are not who God says you are. In those moments when your opponents in life want you to believe that you are not what you think you are, you need a place that you can turn to that will instantly remind you of everything that God has declared about you and over your life.

You cannot allow the outcomes of your life to determine who you are and what you are about.

You cannot allow disappointment to have the last say about who you are. You cannot allow rejection to tell you who you have to be. You cannot allow the outcomes of your life to determine who you are and what you are about. There will be times when no one is standing on the sideline cheering you on. There will be times when you are scrambling and struggling to believe what it is that God has said about you because of all the situations that are swirling round about your life. What do you do when you want to crumble under the pressure that is exerting itself ever so strongly from the outside to create a new definition in your life that you could even justify as being the right one?...you go to the place where John had been baptizing; you return to the place of encounter!

The place where John had been baptizing, in your life, is a place that will reconnect with the voice that thundered from the heavens. The place where John had been baptizing is a place that will undoubtedly remind you and refresh you to who God says you are. The place where John had been baptizing is a timeless well that you can return to at will in order to draw strength. It is a necessity for you to have a place, like Jesus, that you can return to in order to be reminded of what the Father has said about you and over you.

It is a necessity for you to have a place, like Jesus, that you can return to in order to be reminded of what the Father has said about you and over you.

Why is it so important to have a place in your life that you know the Father has spoken over you? If you do not have a place that you can recall where you know you have had a real encounter with the Father and He has told you who you are, where did you get your definition? Did it come from a friend? From a parent? From an accomplishment in life that would cause you to believe something about yourself? If this is the case, you need an encounter with the voice of the Father!

You need the Father's voice to give you definition. In Hebrews chapter 11 verse 3 the Bible says, "By faith we understand that the worlds were prepared by the word of God, so that what is seen was not made out of things which are visible."[62] This verse clearly tells us that the world in which we see received its definition by the Word of God, or in another way, by God's speaking. If the world as we know it received its definition and function from God speaking, how much more should we desire that this be the case for our lives?

When the Father speaks to you the truth of who you are, all of the other voices in your life that have been lobbying for preeminence are silenced. When the Father speaks the truth to you, all of the enemy's lies are shattered.

When the Father speaks to you the truth of who you are, all of the other voices in your life that have been lobbying for preeminence are silenced. When the Father speaks the truth to you, all of the enemy's lies are shattered. The Bible says that the power of life and

---

[62] Heb. 11:3, NASB

death are in the tongue.[63] Words have power. Words have creative power. The words that you come into agreement with have creative power in your life. This is why the enemy wants you to come into agreement with words about you that are not the true identity and definition that the Father has spoken over you.

I need to tell you something again right here: You are who God says you are. You are not who the enemy says you are. You are not who the crowds may say you are. You are not the sum total of your failures. You are not just a reflection of years of bad decisions. You are not even the self-appraisal that you come to whenever you look into the mirror. You are who God says you are!

As you are reading this right now, I pray for you in Jesus' name. I pray that you would no longer come into agreement with all that the enemy has been saying to you. I pray that you would believe what it is that God says about you. I pray that you would allow the voice of the Father to give you definition and direction. I pray that every other voice that has been speaking to you and attempting to persuade you and lead you astray would be exposed for what they are right now, and the power of those words would be broken in your life. I pray that you would step into freedom once

---

[63] Prov. 18:21, NKJV

and for all in who it is that the Father has said you are. In Jesus' name, AMEN!

Upon This Rock

Only the revelation of Jesus as the Christ is enough to defeat the gates of Hades. Any other revelation of Jesus will not only fall short, but it will undoubtedly be trumped by the powers of darkness. You can't simply defeat darkness by proclaiming that Jesus is love. Jesus is love, but He is so much more than love. He is the King of all Kings and the Lord of all Lords! Jesus has defeated sin, death, and the grave, and has ascended to the right hand of the Father where He reigns. This is the revelation of Jesus that the gates of Hades cannot overrun.

"Upon this rock I will build my church."[64] I love that Jesus makes it a point to clear up any misunderstanding that the disciples could possibly have moving forward. Please take notice of something for me: Jesus does not say "church" until His disciples say "King." This is the first time in the Gospels that Jesus releases the word "church" from His mouth, and it does not come until the revelation of Him as the Messiah, the King, the promised Savior has come out of the mouth

[64] Matt. 16:18, NIV

of the disciples.[65] This is the rock that Jesus has determined to build His church upon, the revelation of Him as the King.

If Jesus is determined to build His church upon the revelation of Him as the King, I would suggest that we should be too. Our church building efforts do not revolve around having a passionate preacher and a great worship leader. It is not the strength of our graphic designer and social media team that guarantee us a successful church effort. It is not simply having the right types of individuals so that we can appeal to a certain demographic that we desire to reach in a community or region that is the key. Jesus reveals the key to building, or at least successfully building with Jesus, and that is this: You are the Christ, the Son of the Living God.

If Jesus is determined to build His church upon the revelation of Him as the King, I would suggest that we should be too.

What is successful building? What does successful building look like? Are we to consider ourselves successful just because we are drawing big crowds? Should we automatically assume that the works of our

---

[65] From a personal conversation with Robert Gladstone.

hands are successful because of the size of our building program? If these are the ways that you have evaluated your level of success, you are sadly mistaken. Church is about people. A successful church is about people that look and live like Jesus. A successful church body is a body of people that have been formed, and are being formed, into the image of the Son of God.

The power of the church does not rest upon the positions or the programs; it rests upon the people. And those people must carry the revelation of Jesus as the Christ, the Son of the Living God!

Now this does not mean at all that we can just focus on ourselves and ignore the missional realities the church is to give themselves to; not at all. However, you can have missional realities in place with a people that look and live nothing like Jesus. Jesus is the rock, the foundation, the cornerstone, upon which we are to build and do mission.

Many today that are building the church have forgotten that it is all about the people that are involved. I would suggest that you don't have a church until you have people. You can have the right mission statement, the right vision statement, but until you have people, you have nothing to build with. The church is about faces, about real lives, about people.

The church is not powerful because it has the right positions available. The church is not powerful because of the right programs that have been developed. The church is powerful because of the people. The power of the church does not rest upon the positions or the programs; it rests upon the people. And those people must carry the revelation of Jesus as the Christ, the Son of the Living God! You cannot have a powerful church independent of the people that are involved. What would happen if we truly believed this last statement?

Wherever Jesus finds a people that carry the revelation of Him as the Christ, the Son of the Living God, that is the place He is looking to build His church. If you are one that carries this revelation, you can rest assured, Jesus is looking to build with you. When you come into the revelation of Jesus as the Christ, the Son of the Living God, you become a rallying point in the earth for Jesus to build His church. A rallying point? Yes. You become a point in the earth around which God can rally men. God will literally rally lives around you and draw people to you. The church is built upon the lives of men that carry the revelation, not upon systems, but upon the lives of actual people.

Please take a few moments to watch this stirring
video from one of today's most prominent
and powerful voices.

"The Secret Place"

https://vimeo.com/122154270

4

Jesus Above All Else

———∞∞∞———

Matthew 6:33

"But seek first His kingdom and His righteousness, and all these things will be added to you."[66]

In continuing with our incredible account found in
Matthew chapter 16, the next thing that we need
to discuss as we move along in these verses is the
need to prioritize our pursuits. In verse 19 Jesus says,
"I will give you the keys of the kingdom of heaven;
whatever you bind on earth will be bound in heaven,
and whatever you loose on earth will be loosed in
heaven."[67] Now I am not going to attempt to draw
out the deep theological truths that minds way more

[66] Matt. 6:33, NASB
[67] Matt. 16:19, NIV

brilliant than mine have observed and gotten revelation on throughout the ages. I simply want to draw attention to a beautiful truth, and it is this: As revelation increased, equipping increased.

As the revelation of the disciples increased, Jesus installed into their life something that they were not even asking for. What? Yes. This is amazing. As they came into a greater understanding of who Jesus was, they received from Jesus something that they were not even asking for. I would submit to you that when you make the pursuit of Jesus your greatest priority, you will always be properly equipped for every season of life.

Isn't this what Jesus has already communicated, "But seek first His kingdom and His righteousness, and all these things will be added to you"?[68] When you make seeking Jesus and desiring the person of Jesus your greatest pursuit, all of these *other things* will be added to you. Other things? The disciples received *other things* as they came into greater understanding of who Jesus was.

You have to come to a place in your life where you desire Jesus more than anything else this life has to offer. All of the other pleasures and pursuits that this life avails to you fail miserably in comparison to the beauty of Jesus. The world and all of its attractions

---

[68] Matt. 6:33, NASB

and persuasions must never be allowed to eclipse the radiance of the Son. Jesus was, is, and will always be the grandest of all treasures to be apprehended by those who seek Him diligently with their whole heart.

Jesus was, is, and will always be the grandest of all treasures to be apprehended by those who seek Him diligently with their whole heart.

Jesus has to become greater to you than your pursuit of power. You have to come to the place in your life where you want Jesus more than you want the ministry. Jesus wants to be of greater importance to you than the platforms and the prestige. Is He? Can you honestly say that right now Jesus is what you want more than anything else? When all of your motives are laid bare before the Lord, will they be found pure?

At times we try to fool Jesus with the old Solomon trick. What is the Solomon trick, you ask? Solomon was the son of David and a powerful king in the Old Testament. Solomon was also filled with incredible wisdom. In fact, Solomon did not just have incredible wisdom, but the Bible says, "Solomon's wisdom surpassed the wisdom of all the sons of the east and all the wisdom of Egypt."[69] Wow, that's awesome,

---

[69] 1 Kings 4:30, NASB

but how did Solomon get so wise? God appeared to Solomon at night in a dream and asked him a very important question, "Ask for whatever you want me to give you."[70] Solomon answers God in verses 6 through 9, and in verse 9 he makes his request known to God by saying, "So give your servant a discerning heart to govern your people and to distinguish between right and wrong. For who is able to govern this great people of yours?"[71]

Seems pretty cut and dried up to this point, right? I think so. The point to which we need to look is at what happens next. Over the next couple of verses is where God begins to outline to Solomon what He will now do for Solomon even though he was not asking for it. In verse 10 the Bible speaks of God's pleasure with Solomon because of what it is that he asked for, and then beginning in verse 11 God continues His response and says, "Since you have asked for this and not for long life or wealth for yourself, nor have asked for the death of your enemies but for discernment in administering justice, I will do what you have asked. I will give you a wise and discerning heart, so that there will never have been anyone like you, nor will there ever be. Moreover, I will give you what you have not

---

[70] 1 Kings 3:5, NIV
[71] 1 Kings 3:9, NIV

asked for—both wealth and honor—so that in your lifetime you will have no equal among kings."[72]

I will give you what you have not asked for… sound familiar? There are many things that are incredibly profound about this portion of Scripture that we could make entire discussions about: how God appeared to Solomon in the middle of the night in a dream; the humility of God to come to a man and allow him to request whatever his heart desires; and many more. However, as it relates to the Solomon trick, I did not forget, this is what I mean:

God knows the desires of our hearts and what it is that we really want whenever we come to Him; He sees right through us.

Solomon asked for wisdom, and because of that, God gave him wealth and fame. Today, because what we really want is wealth and fame, we ask for wisdom. The only issue with this is that God knows our hearts. God knows our motives. God knows the desires of our hearts and what it is that we really want whenever we come to Him; He sees right through us.

I have the wonderful privilege of being a father. I have a daughter, a son, and another little girl that we are waiting for her arrival in a few months. My oldest,

---

[72] 1 Kings 3:11-13, NIV

my little girl, has just turned five. My heart has been absolutely wrecked, in the best way possible, from the first time we locked eyes in the hospital delivery room a few years ago. There is something very special about the daddy/daughter bond. My daughter knows that she can come to Daddy and that Daddy will attempt to move heaven and earth to get to her whatever it is that she is asking for.

With all of this being said, there is also something else that is very true. My daughter is now getting to the place where she is beginning to realize that certain things in life she is actually able to leverage that will assist her in greater ways to getting things that she really wants. For instance, there will be times when I will be sitting in one of the chairs in our living room reading and my daughter will come from wherever she is in the house and run up to me and just hug me and hold onto me for a little bit. She then looks up at Daddy with her beautiful blue eyes and smiles big. With a super cute voice she will say to me, "Daddy, I love you so much." By this time I have melted into the chair. Any parent out there knows what these moments are like that I am describing. Well, what I have noticed lately is that from time to time these moments are now followed by something like this, "Dad, can I have some ice cream?" Or, "Dad, can I have some chocolate?"

It is in these moments that I am describing that I am beginning to realize that the way she runs to me and loves on me for a few moments is coming with an ulterior motive; there is an agenda at work here. The flattery and the buttering up are just a setup. The buttering up is a way for her to prime the pump so that she can go in for the kill. The lovey-dovey stuff is just a way for her to maximize the moment and leverage her way into a more effective position for Dad to say yes and grant her true wishes.

Have you ever been in a position where someone was interacting with you and you could tell that they had another motive? Have you ever been in a place where someone was being nice to you, flattering you, attempting to love you, saying really nice things to you, and you did not feel right because you knew that this was not just an end to itself? If you have, you know that it does not feel that great. There is a tendency to feel used.

I want you to stop for a moment if you would and consider if there is any time that you can possibly remember where maybe you have acted like this with your heavenly Father? Has there ever been a time where you thought, *Maybe if I just go in and worship for a little bit…maybe if I spend some extra time in prayer over the next couple of days…maybe if I give a little extra in the offering this week and next week…maybe if I get up extra early all week and read more of my Bible.* All the while it is not really Jesus that we are after, but rather, like my daughter running up to me and loving on me for a little bit, we are really after the ice cream; what we really want is the chocolate.

What does the ice cream and chocolate represent in your life? What is it that deep down inside you really want from Jesus that you think He will give you if you butter Him up or flatter Him with your behavior? Is it the promotion at your job? Is it a position in the ministry? Is it greater influence? Whatever it is that you are really prioritizing as your pursuit, and attempting to use your love for Jesus to get there, I would like to let you in on a little secret…He already knows, and He sees right through it.

What a beautiful place it is to be when the person of Jesus has become our greatest fascination. What an awesome thing it is to declare with the old hymn writer, "Take the world, but give me Jesus."[73] As I said before, seeking Jesus and making the person of Jesus your primary pursuit in life will always equip you for every season of life. We don't seek Him for the equipping; we seek Him because He is worthy of being sought after. We seek Him with our whole heart

---

[73] "Take the World, but Give Me Jesus," by Fanny J. Crosby, Hymnary.org, http://www.hymnary.org/text/take_the_world_but_give_me_jesus_all_its.

and entirety of our life because He alone is the One worthy to ask this of men and women; no one else has offered their perfect life for us; Jesus alone is worthy.

An increase in revelation gave the disciples authorization. They gained authority when they increased in revelation. A greater understanding of Jesus in their life opened up to them a greater place of equipping. Jesus gave them what they did not even realize they needed. Jesus equipped them with what they were not even discerning enough to pray for.

There will be many who go chasing after power. There will be many who go chasing after platforms. Many will chase prestige. Some will chase money. Some will chase acceptance into the right social and professional circles. All of these are lesser pursuits. All of these, even if acquired, will leave you empty and unfulfilled if your life is void **Keep in mind that if you come to Him for any other reason than Him, you will miss Him.** of Jesus. Seek first the Kingdom and His righteousness. Seek first Jesus and His presence. Yet, keep in mind that if you come to Him for any other reason than Him, you will miss Him.

If placed in the position that Solomon found himself, God coming to you and asking you to ask Him of anything, what do you say? What would be the desperate cry of your heart? What words would your lips release if you had the opportunity of a lifetime to ask Almighty God for whatever it is that you truly desired? Would you be able to find it within yourself to ask, with pure intention, for the presence and person of Jesus? Do you really desire Jesus above all else?

There is one who was before Solomon, David, Solomon's father to be specific, who cried out in the psalms, "One thing I have asked from the Lord, that I shall seek: That I may dwell in the house of the Lord all the days of my life, to behold the beauty of the Lord and to meditate in His temple."[74] The burning passion of David's heart was that he would seek the very face of the Lord. A few verses after the one we just read David says, "When you said, 'Seek My face,' my heart said to You, 'Your face, O Lord, shall I seek.'"[75]

"My heart said to you" is what David penned in the psalms. Why is this worth mentioning? For this purpose: is your heart in alignment with the words that come out of your mouth? At times our mouth will release things that our heart does not really believe or fully buy into because, in the moment, what comes out of our mouth is serving a purpose. Maybe it's a nice comment about somebody that we really don't

---

[74] Ps. 27:4, NASB
[75] Ps. 27:8, NASB

believe. Maybe it's a statement that we let go, or agree with, just to get out of a tough situation. Sometimes we think it is easier just to say something to get out of an awkward, or tough, moment because we realize that revealing the true condition of what our heart believes would just cause more tension or trouble. At times we will say with our mouth something that we know we don't believe in our heart.

David said that his heart was crying out for the presence of God. What is it that your heart is crying out for? When truly examined, what is it that you want more than anything else in this life? In consideration of what your answer to this question would be, it is good to also consider the truth that we will always personify our pursuits. You will always be able to look from the outside in at a person's life and visibly see what is most important to them, what their primary pursuit in life is. There are many revealers for this point: how you spend your time, how you spend your money, etc.

You will always be able to look from the outside in at a person's life and visibly see what is most important to them, what their primary pursuit in life is.

As we close this chapter, I ask you again, not just for the sake of repetition, although I do firmly believe that repetition in this scenario has a profound way of chipping away at the rough exterior of our hearts and bringing us to a place of transparency, if you could have God give you one thing in this life, what would it be?

Please take a few moments to watch this stirring
video from one of today's most prominent
and powerful voices.

"Jesus: Life's Greatest Prize; Life's Greatest Pursuit"

https://vimeo.com/122156978

5

Maturing in the Conversation

John 15:15

> "No longer do I call you slaves, for the slave does not know what his master is doing; but I have called you friends, for all things that I have heard from my Father I have made known to you."[76]

U p until this point we have been together on an amazing journey through some passages of Scripture found in the book of Matthew chapter 16. I would like to continue right where we left off last chapter, this time moving forward one verse, to verse

---

[76] John 15:15, NASB

21. Verse 21 says this, "From that time on Jesus began to explain to his disciples that he must go to Jerusalem and suffer many things at the hands of the elders, the chief priests and the teachers of the law, and that he must be killed and on the third day be raised to life."[77] The verse does not really seem to have a right fit with all of the other things that have been happening up until this point. The conversation between Jesus and the disciples seems to have just now intensified for some reason. There does not seem to be anything that they have been discussing up until this point, or any significant event that has happened, that would warrant this type of talk from Jesus. Seems pretty odd…or does it?

I love the wording that the Bible gives us at the beginning of verse 21: *From that time on.* Please just don't read over the first couple of words at the beginning of this verse and miss the fact that it is packed with an incredible amount of meaning. From that time on? From what time on? And what is it that Matthew is writing in here or attempting to draw our attention to?

Matthew is very intentional to tell us that *from that time on* Jesus began to talk to the disciples about certain things. *From that time on* is interesting language because it gives the impression that there has been a change

---

[77] Matt. 16:21, NIV

of some sort; it is transitional language. Something has now shifted. Something is now different. There has been a fulfillment or something has been accomplished that now allows for the progression into something else, something new. *From that time on* tells us that something has now been completed.

In the book of Galatians, chapter 4, the apostle Paul in writing to the church at Galatia tells them, "When the time came to completion, God sent his Son, born of a woman, born under the law...."[78] *When the time came to completion*, to me, sounds like another way to say *from that time on*. When the time was just right, not a moment to soon, and definitely not being late, God sent His Son. In this same fashion, when the moment was just right, not a moment too soon, and definitely not entering it in too late, Jesus began to have a certain talk with the disciples; they were now ready for what it is that Jesus had to tell them. But what is it exactly that made them ready?

From that time on...again, from what time on? We have to look back over a few verses to see what significant thing has happened that would warrant this statement from the writer. Well, just a few verses back to where we started is Jesus walking into a certain region...then turning and asking the disciples some

---

[78] Gal. 4:4, HCSB

questions…and then Peter responding with a revelation that he has just received from the Father, who is in heaven, about who Jesus is…wait! Could that be it? Could that be the significant thing Jesus was waiting for in order for this shift to take place? Could it be that He was awaiting the moment for the disciples to come into a revelation of His person that the Father was unveiling to Peter? I believe so, and I believe it is more important than we know.

Jesus is waiting to reveal certain things about His purpose to you, but it will not come before you have a greater understanding of His person.

Jesus waited until Peter came up in his revelation in order to come up in the significance of what He was willing to talk to them about. I would submit to you at this point this truth: There are certain things that Jesus will not talk to you about until your revelation of who He is increases… and comes up. Jesus is waiting to reveal certain things about His purpose to you, but it will not come before you have a greater understanding of His person. As the knowledge of the person increases, so will the unveiling of that person's purpose; and that person being Jesus, the Son of the living God.

From that time on Jesus began to reveal to them…I want to make this as clear as possible because this is something that you cannot afford to miss. This one truth could be the difference between your spending the rest of your life doing good things that come from good ideas that you continue to generate and invest your life into, or doing God things that are heaven sent, Spirit led, and God fulfilled. I don't know about you, but I want my life to count. I want my life to mark my generation. I want my life to be filled with meaning and purpose, God's purpose! Jesus would not talk to them about certain things until they came into greater understanding of who He was. He would not reveal His purpose until His person was first revealed.

It is imperative that we as believers be connected to what it is that God is doing today in the earth, what God is doing in our generation. God has chosen for you to be alive right now. You were not chosen to live one hundred years ago. God did not choose for you to be born back in AD 200; you are alive right now! You have been selected by God to be alive at such a time as this. I think it should be important to us that if God has put us right here, right now, we should be desirous to know what the Father is doing.

The conversation has now shifted with the disciples and they have been brought into the talk of what the Father is doing. What was God doing in the day that the disciples lived? *From that time on* Jesus began to tell them what the Father was doing. God, in the person of Jesus, was headed to Jerusalem to suffer, be killed, and be raised; that is what God was doing in their day. Jesus was waiting until the shift in revelation happened so that He could shift the conversation.

I think it is amazing that Jesus would entrust to them the revelation of what He was up to. I find it to be astonishing that Jesus would be willing to unveil the heart and purposes of the Father to those that walked with Him. The Father was, and is, willing to let us in on what He is doing. As our revelation of Jesus matures, so will the conversations that Jesus will have with us; it is a natural part of maturing.

As our revelation of Jesus matures, so will the conversations that Jesus will have with us; it is a natural part of maturing.

A natural part of the process of maturing in life is the types, or content, of talks you are willing to have with someone or be on the receiving end of. You would not have the same type of conversation with a two-year-old that you would with a twelve-year-old. In the same way you would not have a conversation with a twelve-year-old that you would with a twenty-year-old. You could obviously talk to a forty-two-year-old about different things that a twenty-two-year-old may not be ready for or be able to relate to. In this case, the determining factor is not age; it is revelation, or capacity, if you would.

Your current revelation could be viewed as a container. Depending on the size of the container will directly determine what you are able to pour into that container. Obviously if you had a small container you would not attempt to put something too large into it for concern that it would go to waste because the container would not be able to bear the load of what was being input, or installed. If you were to speak to the container you may say something like this: "I have much more for you, just more than you are now able to bear." Does this sound familiar? It should. I think you need to hear the words of Jesus in the book of John as He is speaking to the disciples, "There is so much more that I want to tell you, but you can't bear it now."[79]

We need to realize that it is not unwillingness on the part of Jesus that He will not share certain things with us yet. The verse we just read from the book of John clearly reveals that Jesus is very willing to share things with us. He just will not pour those things into a container that does not have the capacity to bear what is being installed, or poured in. We must be jealous for an increase in capacity! We must be

---

[79] John 16:12, NLT

jealous for an increase in revelation. We must be jealous to know Jesus!

I would suggest to you that you could determine what your capacity is by the type of talks Jesus is willing to have with you. What type of talks has Jesus been having with you? Is it time for some maturing in the talk? Is it time for an increase in capacity? You will be the only one that can honestly know if this is the case. Will you be honest enough with yourself to answer? If not, there are issues that await you.

Let me let you in on a simple truth: God will not entrust to you anything that is larger than your current revelation of His Son.

It is definitely a problem when we desire more responsibility without first coming into greater revelation. It is an issue when we want to be entrusted with more purpose without first coming into more of an understanding about the person. Many want more authority, but they don't have a concern to pursue the One who authorizes men in the earth. Let me let you in on a simple truth: God will not entrust to you anything that is larger than your current revelation of His Son.

When the disciples came into a greater revelation of Jesus, they were given more responsibility. Responsibility comes with revelation. Not just that we are simply given things to do, but there is a greater level of accountability to now steward the revelation of Jesus that we have received. When was the last time you knew that you came into an increase in your revelation of Jesus?

Let us never grow weary in our relational pursuit of the man, Christ Jesus. One thing that is very damaging to a relationship is when one person becomes familiar enough with the other that they feel they have them all figured out. When you feel as if you have someone all figured out, your motivation to continue to pursue that person begins to diminish. Inquisitiveness and fascination deplete the more you think you know someone.

This common fact should not be the case in our walk with Jesus, in our pursuit of Christ. Jesus is an endless revelation. Jesus is the same yesterday, today, and forever; however, He is new every morning! Again, as we have already discussed, here we will insert again our need for the Holy Spirit continually working in our life to make the reality of Jesus known to us day by day.

Jesus is the same yesterday, today, and forever; however, He is new every morning!

Jesus wants to be known. Jesus is desperate to make Himself known to you. This is not an intense game of manhunt where Jesus has found the greatest hiding place and is forever going to laugh at you while you attempt to find Him. Revelation, in fact, should not even be viewed as an end to itself, but more as a starting place, a doorway, a sign that says to you: run this way; come and find more of me here!

Maybe you feel as if you have gotten a good grasp on who Jesus is and what it is that He is all about. If that is the case, I pray for a fire to flood your heart right now with an intense desire for Jesus. I pray that you would come into a season of hunger that is greater than anything you have ever known. I pray for something more than what you yourself are able to manage. I pray for a longing so strong, so real, and so genuine, that you would not be able to satisfy it with any of the lesser things that have always done the job before. I pray for Jesus to become more real to you. I pray for you to become connected to what the Father is doing in your day. It is time for your revelation to mature. It is time for the conversation to mature!

Please take a few moments to watch this stirring
video from one of today's most prominent
and powerful voices.

"Connected to the Father's Heart"

https://vimeo.com/122157079

6

Dead to Self?

———∞∞∞———

"When Christ calls a man, he bids him to come
and die."   —Dietrich Bonhoeffer[80]

We have now reached an interesting part of
our journey. Jesus has just begun to reveal
to the disciples a greater depth of His purposes; He
has opened their eyes to that which He is doing in
the earth. At this point, Peter, who just a few verses
ago had the life-changing revelation that Jesus is the
Christ, the Son of the Living God, speaks up again to
Jesus; only this time Peter speaks up to rebuke Jesus
for the way that He is talking now. Peter rebukes

---

[80] "Dietrich Bonhoeffer Was Hanged Today," by John Piper,
desiringGod blog, http://www.desiringgod.org/articles/dietrich-
bonhoeffer-was-hanged-today.

Jesus? Seriously? Yes, seriously. There was obviously something about what Jesus was saying that Peter did not agree with or like all that much.

After Jesus finishes telling the disciples that He is headed to Jerusalem to lay down His life, Peter pulls Jesus aside and says, "Never, Lord!" "This shall never happen to you!"[81] Now this is where the plot begins to thicken. Jesus does not just let what Peter has to say slide. Jesus has an immediate response for Peter's contribution to the conversation. Jesus looks at Peter and says, "Get away from me, Satan! You are a dangerous trap to me. You are seeing things merely from a human point of view, not from God's."[82]

Get away from me, Satan? Really? Is Jesus delusional? Has Jesus just temporarily lost His bearings and forget where He was and who He was surrounded by? Surely Satan could not have been anywhere around for Jesus to make this type of statement in response to Peter's loving concern for Jesus losing His life…or could he?

There is something that is critical for us to make sure we catch here before we move on to the next couple of verses in this section. Let's simplify things so that we can make very plain what is happening here. The disciples have just come into a greater revelation

---

[81] Matt. 16:22, NIV
[82] Matt. 16:23, NLT

of Jesus. When their revelation increases, Jesus begins to share with them a greater depth of His work and purposes in the earth. A part of this greater purpose and work that Jesus is doing involves Him willingly walking into Jerusalem where He already knows that He will be handed over, mistreated, beaten and bloodied beyond belief, and ultimately killed, and then raised on the third day.

Feeding the poor and multiplying food for the multitudes? Surely there was too much work left to be done for You to just end it all here by walking into Jerusalem and handing Yourself over to death.

I know that it must have confounded the minds of the disciples to hear Jesus talking about journeying toward Jerusalem knowing that when He arrived there this terrible process that He had just finished detailing to them would begin to unfold. Why would He willingly give Himself to such a process? Does not it make more sense to stay clear of Jerusalem in order to continue preaching about the Kingdom of God? Wouldn't't it be a better use of Your time and life that You have left to invest it healing the sick? Raising the dead? Feeding the poor and multiplying food for the multitudes? Surely there was too much work left to be done for You to just end it all here by walking into Jerusalem and handing Yourself over to death.

Peter and the rest of the disciples would have also been familiar with the prophetic promises that were wrapped up in their hopes of Jesus being the Messiah. The disciples would have heard the stories passed down from generation to generation that one day God would return, and **Jesus represents the** not just return, but would **freedom that the** mightily return to rescue **disciples know has** His people out of bondage **been promised, not** and captivity. The bondage **just by men, but** of the Roman Empire **also by God.** would have been a yoke that the disciples and the rest of the people found themselves under and would have been something that, if the Messiah should come in their day, they would excitedly await deliverance from. Jesus represents the freedom that the disciples know has been promised, not just by men, but also by God Himself. This freedom surely can't be achieved if Jesus is talking about going into Jerusalem and handing Himself over to die.

With all of the hopes and dreams that are wrapped up in Jesus, with all of the promises yet to be fulfilled wrapped up in the man that stands before them, with the end of the oppression so close, Jesus' talk of giving

Himself over to death is something that just absolutely does not makes sense to Peter. Somebody has to do something about this. Somebody has to remind Jesus of what is all riding on the line here. Surely someone will step up and return Jesus to His right senses so that He will stop all of this foolish talk about death, and not just death as in someone chasing Him down and killing Him, but willingly walking into the place that will begin the process that will result in the end of His life. Surely someone will do something!

Peter decides that the someone who is going to have to put their foot down and bring things back is... him, and this is where he pulls Jesus aside and attempts to confront this absurdity flowing from Jesus' lips. Now, rather than Jesus snapping out of it and realizing the significance of the moment and returning to His right senses, He makes an extremely bold statement in return: "Get away from me, Satan!"[83] I wonder what the look on Peter's face must have looked like when these words came out of Jesus' mouth directed at him. These words had to have been like the sharpest of arrows that viciously pierced the heart of Peter when they were released from the lips of Jesus. There are a lot of bad things that you can call a person, but to have God in the flesh look at you face-to-face and call you

---

[83] Matt. 16:23, NLT

Satan, this surely is not the outcome that Peter was hoping for.

As if this was not bad enough, Jesus continues with another short power-packed statement in response to Peter's concern for Him. Jesus says, "You are a dangerous trap to me. You are seeing things merely from a human point of view, not from God's."[84] A dangerous trap? This is Peter, the disciple that Jesus had called away from all things in order to walk with Him. This is Peter, one of the twelve that Jesus had hand selected to do life with Him and be personally invested into. How could Peter all of a sudden become Satan and a dangerous trap all in the same sentence? Jesus gives us the validation for these remarks in the last portion of His response, "You are seeing things merely from a human point of view, not from God's."

This may seem a little harsh to you. You may have a hard time reconciling the love that Jesus has for His disciples and the response that He issues to Peter. Let's clear up some of this confrontation because there are key points that we will not want to miss about Peter's loving concern for Jesus and then Jesus' seemingly rash comeback to Peter. There is something happening beneath the surface of this exchange, and this is why Jesus will not just allow this rebuke from

---

[84] Matt. 16:23, NLT

Peter and the following comments to just slip away without making it a point to put an end to what is attempting to rise up in the moment.

Let's back up for just a moment. Peter says to Jesus, "Never, Lord! Surely this will never happen to you!" Again, this does not seem that bad. This is coming from a man that had truly abandoned all earthly things to follow after this Jesus that stood before him. This was a man that no longer considered what he had in the world to be of more value than the opportunity to walk with Jesus. This was a man that wanted to see Jesus victorious…and victory surely could not be won by willingly giving yourself over to death. But you see, what Peter did not realize is that what Jesus was looking for was in fact death; a death to self is what would be required for those who would come after Jesus. Jesus was modeling before them what He would eventually expect from them—total surrender.

Jesus was modeling before them what He would eventually expect from them—total surrender.

I do not want to make it seem as if Peter is someone that we should look down upon in this story, which is definitely not the case and certainly not what I am suggesting we are to do. I am sure that any of us standing with Jesus on that day would have done the same thing, or at least thought about doing the same thing for sure, even if we did not actually find the bravery to pull Him aside and rebuke Him. Peter is not one that we should frown upon here; he is in a process of learning and growing as we all are as we are walking with Jesus. This is a perfect opportunity for Jesus to make a stand. There has to be a distinction made between what is acceptable moving forward and what is not. There is a mind-set that Jesus wanted rooted out of Peter, a mind-set that is deadly enough to prevent them from ever truly becoming all that Jesus knew they could be.

Peter carries the revelation of Jesus as the Christ, the Son of the Living God. Yet, at the same time Peter apparently carries an unwillingness to allow Jesus to hand Himself over to death? Why? Again, all that Peter hoped for was wrapped up in Jesus remaining alive and with them. All that had been promised was encapsulated in this Man that stood with them. But Jesus does not just speak to Peter as if he was making an error in love; he combines the name Satan and thinking with human concerns only. What is the connection here?

Death is the ultimate fear of life. The fear of death is greater than arachnophobia, the fear of spiders. The fear of death is greater than achluophobia, the fear of the dark. The fear of death is also greater than coulrophobia, the fear of clowns. Yes, there is an actual phobia for those who are afraid of clowns. I am sure that death was not something that was at the front of Peter's mind as he was traveling with Jesus and watching Him defeat sin, sickness, and even death itself. Remember, Jesus raised Lazarus from the grave.[85] How could Jesus give Himself to something that He apparently had power over?

In order to truly understand the severity of Jesus' response to Peter we have to look not only at the verses that we have in mention here, but at the next couple of verses also. Listen to all that Jesus says to those standing with Him at the moment over the next couple of verses, "If anyone wishes to come after Me, he must deny himself, and take up his cross and follow Me. For whoever wants to save his life will lose it; but whoever loses his life for My sake will find it. For what will it profit a man if he gains the whole world yet forfeits his soul? Or what will a man give in exchange for his soul?"[86]

Aha! Now we are getting to the issue at hand. Now we have had the curtain pulled back and are able to really see and hear what it is that triggered this type of statement from Jesus in response to Peter. Jesus looks at all of the disciples and explains to them that anyone who wants to come after Him must deny himself and

---

[85] John 11:43, NIV
[86] Matt. 16:24-26, NASB

be willing to lose his life. There is no room for self-preservation where Jesus is going. There is no room for love of self to the point that you would be unwilling to deny yourself and lay down your life where Jesus is leading. The exaltation of self above the purposes of God is something that must be laid down in order to follow Jesus. Again, Jesus is modeling the expectation for all; this is not an unrealistic expectation that He Himself is not willing to walk out, and in fact, is walking out before their very eyes.

The exaltation of self above the purposes of God is something that must be laid down in order to follow Jesus.

Not loving your life sounds familiar. Revelation says, "They triumphed over him by the blood of the Lamb and the word of their testimony; they did not love their lives so much as to shrink from death."[87] There is a denial of self that must be in place in order to walk where Jesus is walking. Peter was not ready for this type of talk. Jesus was riding a great wave of momentum. His testimony was rising in the region and there was great fame being attached to His movement.[88] How could what Jesus has just described to them be the way the story ends?

---

[87] Rev. 12:11, NIV
[88] Luke 4:14, JUB

The Bible tells us that the mouth speaks what the heart is full of.[89] Peter carries the revelation of Jesus, but at the same time carries an unwillingness to lay his life down. It is this unwillingness that Peter tries to transfer onto the life of Jesus, and Jesus would have nothing to do with it. It is this issue that Jesus speaks to. It is this unwillingness that Jesus identifies as being a characteristic of Satan's influence. It is this unwillingness that Jesus points out as thinking with human concerns only.

We know that Satan was thrown down out of heaven. Why? Satan wanted to exalt himself above God.[90] Satan had pride that would not allow him to bow to God and deny himself. Satan had a sense of self-preservation and self-exaltation that took priority over submission to God's authority. These are the characteristics that Jesus sniffed out in Peter's seemingly loving concern for His willingness to lay His life down. Jesus is quick to speak to this and clear up any misunderstanding before they take one more step. Jesus knows this absolutely must be dealt with.

Again, let's not be quick to jump Peter's case for what is happening here. Before we look down upon Peter, let's be clear about something: This is not something that just has to be dealt with in Peter; this is

---

[89] Luke 6:45, NIV
[90] Isa. 14:12-14, ESV

something that must be dealt with in all of us. All of us? Yes, all of us…you read that right. This is not some side issue that you can attempt to sidestep because you think that you are in the clear.

Jesus said that if any man were going to follow after Him, he must first deny himself. Any man. Any man means that it does not matter what kind of social status you have. Any man means it does not matter how many followers you have on Twitter. It does not matter how many friends you have on Facebook or how many likes you have on Instagram. It does not matter the size of your bank account. It does not matter how gifted you are. It does not matter how qualified you may feel, or how unqualified. Any man means exactly what Jesus is saying here…any man!

Any man that would come after me *must* deny himself. This is not a suggestion. This is not some cute little recommendation that Jesus is throwing out there to those standing with Him that day; this is a matter of life and death. Life and death? Really? Yes. There is a death that is required and a life that needs to be infused. This is actually a beautiful invitation more than it is a gruesome requirement.

The invitation is for Jesus Himself to come alive in those who would die to themselves. Jesus will only stand up inside of a man that is willing to lie down. Jesus will not compete for which one of you will stand tall. This laying down that is being asked of you is not something that you are able to accomplish in your own strength. This laying down is only possible through the grace of God. Of the many things that the grace of God is, one key component is this: empowerment to lay your life down.

Of the many things that the grace of God is, one key component is this: empowerment to lay your life down.

In the next chapter we will discuss the grace of God in greater detail just so that we are clear as we move forward with what exactly grace is and what it is intended to produce in the lives of believers. Jesus surely issues grace, but not without a purpose. In the same way that Jesus offered His life with a purpose, grace has been given with a purpose. We will examine that purpose next!

Please take a few moments to watch my video and continue to be challenged on what it truly means to:

"Entrust Yourself to the Grave"

https://vimeo.com/122181299

7

Grace on Purpose

———⚬⚬⚬———

Grace:

1. Unmerited Favor

2. Empowerment

Grace: Empowerment to live like and look like Jesus.

It is an absolute necessity for any that desire to be conformed to the image of the Son that we understand what grace is and what it is all about. It takes a wholehearted dependency in and on the grace of God in order for this life in Christ to be successful. In other words, you cannot do it on your own. This life in Christ is not something that you can produce in your own might. God is not after the best version of yourself that you are able to produce. He wants to conform you to the image of His Son, and for this, it cannot be accomplished without the grace of God.

Grace is mentioned in the Scriptures several times; in fact, grace is mentioned 157 times in the Bible.[91] Of the 157 times that it is mentioned, most are translated to mean what many are comfortable with as a definition, and that would be: unmerited favor.[92] Unmerited favor is something that we are comfortable receiving because it means that I was unworthy and God decided to give me something that I really did not deserve. This is incredible and much needed for sure. However, there is another definition of grace that is translated and I feel is key to what we are discussing here. The other translation of the word grace in the Bible is: Empowerment. Unmerited favor is easy; it means that God does it all. Empowerment is not so easy; it means that God empowers me to do something.

What is it that God would consider empowering me to do? In the book of Hebrews chapter 4 we find a perfect example of the dual meaning of grace. Hebrews chapter 4 verse 16 says, "Therefore, let us draw near with confidence to the throne of *grace*, so that we may

---

[91] *Strong's Concordance*, Bible Hub, http://biblehub.com/greek/5485. htm.

[92] Ibid., *Strong's Concordance*, 5485.

receive mercy and find *grace* to help in time of need."[93] The first use of grace in this verse means that we come to God to find unmerited favor. The second, however, is not translated unmerited favor; it is translated empowerment. God undoubtedly is looking to empower His people.

God's desire is to empower a people to live and look like Jesus. The book of Romans tells us that God's desire, His pre-thought of our life, is that we would be conformed to the image of His Son, Jesus.[94] Any grace that I receive that does not cause me to look and live more like Jesus

Grace is not something that is supposed to be self-centered; it is Jesus-centered.

is not grace that is being issued from God Himself. I am leery of any message of grace that does not call me to abandon the pursuit of myself to be empowered in the process of being conformed to the image of the Son. Grace is not something that is supposed to be self-centered; it is Jesus-centered.

Grace is not self-centered. Grace is not self-centered because grace is not empowerment for the "I" in our life. Grace is not the empowerment for the "I" to live. It is empowerment for the "I" to be surrendered so that the Son of God by the power of the

---

[93] Heb. 4:16, NASB (emphasis added is mine)
[94] Rom. 8:29, NASB

Holy Spirit can be formed in you. The pursuit of the "I" in our life has to be surrendered and put to death in order for the life of Jesus to be formed in us. God will not compete with you over who you desire to reflect. The goal of it all is so that when men see you, they see the life of Jesus.

The pursuit of the "I" in our life has to be surrendered and put to death in order for the life of Jesus to be formed in us.

The apostle Paul was a man who understood that the pursuit of the "I" in his life had to come to an end in order for the life of the Son of God to be formed in him. It was Paul himself who said, "I have been crucified with Christ; it is no longer "I" who live, but Christ lives in me; and the life I now live in the flesh I live by faith in the Son of God, who loved me and gave Himself up for me."[95] This is the cry of a man who actually got it. He understood that the life that God was calling him to live was not going to be possible without the grace of God.

We need to come to the place in our life where we confront the hard truth that, even with our best intentions and efforts that we put forth, we cannot produce in this life what God is looking for out of us. God does

---

[95] Gal. 2:20, NASB (emphasis added is mine)

not say that His desire is to conform us to the image of His Son so that we can run around giving it everything we have got in an attempt to make that happen the best way we know how. Even if you could produce a good image of Jesus in your life yourself, God would not be satisfied, nor would He be pleased. The book of Isaiah lets us know that all of our own righteousness is like filthy rags to God.[96] Paul understood this truth very well, and for it, he chose to wholeheartedly lean upon God's grace that would cause him to be what he could never be on his own.

Richard Wurmbrand said it this way about the apostle Paul, "Not I live, not the old I, not the new I, but Christ lives in me; the I has been abolished."[97] Has the pursuit of the "I" in your life been abolished? God is not after you looking like the best version of you that you can be. He's after Jesus being formed in you by the power of the Holy Spirit. Don't settle for merely what you are able to produce in this life. I don't care if everyone around you thinks that you are a superstar spiritual person. If you have not fallen completely dependent on the grace of God for Jesus to be formed in your life, you have not gotten what this thing is all about.

---

[96] Isa. 64:6, NIV

[97] "Richard Wurmbrand, Tortured for Christ," by Eric Gilmour, *YouTube,* https://www.youtube.com/watch?v=Tz9kctO_b6M.

Richard Wurmbrand said not the old I, and not the new I, but it is Christ now that lives in me. Hear this, because it is easy to read over that line and miss what he is actually communicating to us through these words. We would all agree that the old I is no longer an issue when we come to Christ; we are all going to amen that statement whenever it is made. Take off the old man.[98] Lay down your old sinful ways. Submit the life that you used to live to God. The old has passed away, all things have become new.[99] But the verse Richard uses just does not mention the old "I." He also says, "And not the new 'I.'"

I would suggest that there is just as much possible bondage with the new you as there is attached to the old you.

For the most part we get the initial portion of this verse; it is no longer the old "I" that lives. I have rid myself of the old me by surrendering my life to Christ. By laying my life down at the feet of Jesus I have been set free from the old me. But what about the new me? I would argue that Jesus wants you to be free from the new you also. I would suggest that there is just as much possible bondage with the new you as there is attached to the old you.

[98] Eph. 4:22, KJV
[99] 2 Cor. 5:17, NIV

Again, Jesus is not looking for you to become the best you that you can be without Him. Meaning, there is a tendency to come to Jesus, lose sight of the old man, and now gain a newfound infatuation with the new man. There is a temptation to become satisfied with your new man. There is a trap that makes an idol out of the new man. There is an attempt of the enemy that awaits you that will want you to become so obsessed with your new man that you are now unwilling to lay down this new man because of how spiritual you think you are.

Some will lose sight of the old man, but now they worship their new man. They become self-righteous. They pride themselves in how hard they have worked in order to develop this new man that has now come to the surface of their life. They pride themselves in their spiritual routines; their prayer life; their knowledge of the Scriptures; their freedom in worship…and so on. How you ever stopped to think that Jesus continually wants you to keep this new man laid down also? Again, we are all comfortable with laying down the old man, but what about laying down the new man?

If the enemy cannot get you to go back to your old ways, he will just attempt to get you to form new ways that are minus the life of God that are being sustained by your own strength. The enemy will want you to become infatuated with your new man to the point that you are unwilling to lay it down to Jesus. There is a real place that you can end up, like Peter did, where you feel like you have a lot going for you…where things seem to be heading in all of the right directions…where your gifts are opening doors…where God seems to be using you…and because of all that would seem like circumstantial evidence in your life, you can convince yourself that you have no reason to continue to lay your life down.

To think that I could have one encounter, or experience, with Jesus and then be set forever is absurd.

I encourage you to take a moment and honestly examine your heart. If you are having trouble with the things that I am saying because you feel as if they don't apply to you, I greatly encourage you especially to take a moment and ask yourself these questions: When was the last time I laid my life down to Jesus? When was the last time I surrendered my agenda to the feet of Jesus?

It takes the continual inflow of the life of Jesus in order for us to look like Jesus. This spiritual life cannot be lived successfully without a continual coming. It is not a one quick shot of Jesus and we are good to go for the rest of our days; we have to keep coming, day by day. To think that I could have one encounter, or experience, with Jesus and then be set forever is absurd. When was the last time you knew you met with Him?

If it has been some time ago, you may need to stop reading right now, and in a very simple, yet very real way, close your eyes and say these words out loud: Jesus, I don't want anything but You. I cannot live this life without You. I don't even want to do those things I know I am capable of doing and merely getting by without You. I surrender afresh right now. I lay down my life, again. I surrender my agenda. I just want You. You are more than enough for me. Fill me afresh with the Holy Spirit. In Jesus' name. Amen!

Please take a few moments to watch this stirring
video from one of today's most prominent
and powerful voices.

"The Grace of God"

https://vimeo.com/122181354

8

Without an Agenda and Unapologetic

———— ⚭ ————

Agenda: The underlying intentions or motives of a particular person or group.

Grace is the empowerment to fulfill the invitation of Jesus to deny self and follow Him. It takes Jesus to follow Jesus. We cannot one day simply decide that we are no longer going to look to ourselves. It is not possible without an absolute dependency in and on the grace of God in our lives. Grace is the power to deny self and the empowerment to live like Jesus as we follow after Him and He is formed in us.

Many live a life that is self-absorbed. I would argue that it takes the grace of God to take my eyes off of me and keep them upon Jesus. A man, in and of himself, cannot remove his eyes from his own self without grace. Grace lifts my eyes off of me and locks them upon the Son of God. It takes grace to be able to see Jesus; it takes grace to continue to see Jesus. The same grace that we must have that unveils our eyes to see is the same grace that we are in desperate need of that continues to enable me to see. The truth is that Jesus invites me to deny myself, and then gives me the ability to do so through the empowering of grace working in my life.

It is no secret that Jesus starts at the hardest place for any of us, and that being self-denial. It is outside of our makeup to want to deny self. Because of the original fall and the sin nature that we have inherited, we are born with an innate desire to pursue ourselves, to look out for number one. The pursuit of self is something that Jesus deals with right in the introduction to a life of following after Him; He eliminates the idea that it can exist.

The original invitation to follow after Jesus sounded something like this, "If anyone wishes to come after Me, he must deny himself, and take up his cross and follow Me."[100] I love the way it reads in the New Living Translation, "If any of you wants to be my follower, you must turn from your selfish ways,

---

[100] Matt. 16:24, NASB

take up your cross, and follow me."[101] In other words, right out of the gate Jesus is explicitly saying that there can be no other agenda to following Him other than Him. The selfish agenda of coming to Jesus *for* something is dealt with in the invitation, and the entry part of the invitation is a call to deny.

> **The selfish agenda of coming to Jesus *for* something is dealt with in the invitation, and the entry part of the invitation is a call to deny.**

The definition of denial is this: state that one refuses to admit the truth or existence of; refrain from satisfying oneself; refuse access to. These definitions are powerful when we consider what it is that we are discussing. These definitions give the invitation of Jesus so much more clear, rich meaning. Jesus is asking you to refuse the existence of your own pursuit. Jesus is asking you to refrain from satisfying yourself by pursuing yourself. Jesus is inviting you to refuse access to the life that is built around self-pursuit. Jesus is issuing a summons for all that would be willing to drop their own agenda.

Through the denial of self we are freed up to be about the Father's business. Until we are free from the pursuit of ourselves, we will not be free from the

---

[101] Matt. 16:24, NLT

desire to promote and fulfill our own agenda. We can pray prayers like, "Let Your kingdom come and Your will be done," but until we've been set free from the pursuit of ourselves, we will continue to put our best foot forward in an attempt to see our kingdom built and our will established in the earth. This will happen and express itself in varying degrees, but nonetheless, a man that has not found empowerment to deny himself will always want to promote himself.

Until we are free from the pursuit of ourselves, we will not be free from the desire to promote and fulfill our own agenda.

In fact, there are many in the Scriptures, some that we will examine, who found a way to abandon the pursuit of their own will and desires to be found alive in the purpose of God in the moment. Jesus was a man that did not have an agenda of His own. Jesus told His disciples in the book of John that He came down out of heaven, not to do His own will, but the will of Him who sent Him.[102] I don't think it gets any clearer than that. Jesus told them that day that He was not wandering around the earth in an attempt to fulfill His own desires, but those of His Father who had sent Him. Jesus was a man on a

---

[102] John 6:38, NIV

clear mission; that mission just did not have a personal agenda attached to it.

For God in all His fullness was pleased to live in Christ.[103] What is it that attracts God to install the fullness of who He is into flesh in the earth? The answer is simply profound: a man or woman with no agenda. God looks for a man or woman with no agenda outside of His pursuit. A man or woman with no agenda is a weapon in the hand of God. A man or woman with no agenda is a round set in the chamber that God can fire off into the earth with great precision and purpose that will always hit the mark. A man or woman with no agenda is someone that has walked into the reality that God Himself is our exceeding great reward, like He told Abraham,[104] and all other things that are lived for and pursued in this life pale in comparison to the prize that is His presence.

Many are more aware of their own passions than they are the purposes of God in their life and generation. We need men and women in our day that have died to self and come alive to God. This is radically counterintuitive and countercultural. We need men and women in our day who have encountered Him in such a way that they are dead to themselves for the rest of their days. We need men and women who have been

---

[103] Col. 1:19, NLT
[104] Gen. 15:1, NASB

ruined to the pursuit of self by an encounter with Jesus. One encounter with Jesus is enough to ruin you for the rest of your days. One encounter with Jesus is enough.

As stated before, Jesus was a man that was wholeheartedly submitted to fulfilling the purposes of the Father, yet had no personal agenda of His own. Of all the places this truth is clearly seen, I would like for you to take a look at a story found in the book of Luke, which illustrates this truth beautifully. Luke says this about Jesus beginning in verse 40,

> "And the Child grew and became strong in spirit, filled with wisdom; and the grace of God was upon Him. His parents went to Jerusalem according to the custom of the feast. When they had finished the days, as they returned, the Boy Jesus lingered behind in Jerusalem. And Joseph and His mother did not know it, but supposing Him to have been in the company, they went a day's journey, and sought Him among their relatives and acquaintances. So when they did not find Him, they returned to Jerusalem, seeking Him. Now so it was that after three days they found Him in the temple, sitting in the midst of teachers, both listening to them and asking them questions. And all who heard Him were astonished at His understanding and answers.

So when they saw Him, they were amazed; and His mother said to Him, "Son, why have you done this to us? Look, Your father and I have sought You anxiously." And He said to them, "Why do you seek Me? Did you not know that I must be about My Father's business?" But they did not understand the statement which He spoke to them."[105]

Let's dissect these verses together. Now, again, I am not attempting to pull out all of the wonderful truth that is found in these verses, but, I am definitely pointing toward the truth found that illustrates the point of having no agenda that we are discussing. So, let us begin. In verse 40 we are told that Jesus has grown, become strong in spirit, has been filled with wisdom, and for our purposes in this discussion, a very pivotal point that Luke is intentionally pointing out to us, the grace of God was upon Him. It was this grace that was the setup for the comment that Jesus makes at the end of these verses.

Next, His family has traveled according to the custom of the feasts to Jerusalem. However, when they had finished three days they leave, and somehow make it an entire day away before they realize that

---

[105] Luke 2:40-50, NKJV

Jesus is not with them. What? Any parent knows that this has now turned into a bad situation. Any parent that has ever misplaced a child in a grocery store, shopping mall, amusement park, or anywhere else for that matter, knows that this is not good.

After searching for Jesus for a day among their relatives and company traveling with them, they decide to make their way back toward Jerusalem. This has to be frustrating for them. Jesus is now ruining their plans. They now have to go backwards because they began to move forward and realized that Jesus was not with them where they were going. They leave out of Jerusalem and make it an entire day only to realize that the presence of Jesus is not with them. This is enough of a reason for them to stop their forward progress and do whatever they must in order to regain the presence of Jesus before continuing to their destination.

Let me just say this before we continue. If you have journeyed a day, or even days, and now realize that the presence of Jesus is not with you wherever it is that you are headed, stop everything that you are doing and return to the place that you remember He was last with you. Isn't it odd that we can at times make our own plans without the Presence? Isn't it odd that we can, at times, decide to venture off into our own direction without checking first to make sure that this is somewhere Jesus is willing to walk with me? At times, we can manufacture our own creative wishes, lustful desires, or selfish agendas and begin to run towards them, only to make it however many days out to then realize that the presence of Jesus has not been with us the entire time.

This is no small thing; this is a big deal...a big enough deal for Jesus' parents to stop dead in their tracks and turn around. And where is it that they go? They go back to Jerusalem, because that is where they had Jesus with them last. Maybe today you need to make a conscious decision to stop dead in your tracks. Maybe today is the day when you realize that you have been making plans

Maybe today is the day that you have to turn around and head back to Jerusalem...why? Because that is where Jesus was with you last.

without the Presence. Maybe today is the day that you have to turn around and head back to Jerusalem... why? Because that is where Jesus was with you last.

Now, Luke tells us that it has been three days and they still have not found Jesus. Searching for Him around Jerusalem has not proven to be a successful work. Until they come up on the temple and find Jesus there sitting among the teachers listening and asking questions. Jesus is basically hanging out as if nothing is wrong at the moment. When they find

Him, Jesus' mother goes to Him and asks what I find to be a very appropriate question, "Son, why have you done this to us? Your father and I have been anxiously searching for You."

Being a parent of two little ones and one on the way myself, I can only imagine the emotion that must have been involved in this moment. It has now been three whole days without knowing where my child is or what has happened to him. All of the thoughts that would have wandered through my mind over the course of those days as I frantically searched for my child would have surely been overwhelming. All of the questions that I would have to confront as my continued search went to no avail: Is he safe? Did someone take him? Is he still alive? No parent wants to have to confront these questions about the life of any of their children.

The Bible does not clearly let us in on the emotion that Mary expresses in this exchange with Jesus, but I am sure that this was not a soft, dry question that Mary was asking her Son. But what I would like for you to notice with me is not so much Mary's question, or even the way that Mary asks her question, but look at Jesus' response to what His mother asks Him. We have already set up the situation at hand, so you can probably imagine that Jesus is going to recognize the weight of the moment and lovingly apologize to His parents for what has happened, or at least have some sort of amazing story as to why He did not make it into the company of people that were traveling when His parents decided that it was time to pull out and leave Jerusalem, right? Let's see exactly what Jesus has to say at this point in the story.

Jesus turns to His mother and says these words, "Why do you seek Me? Don't you know that I must be about My Father's business?" What? This does not make sense. Surely Jesus has to understand the frustration that He has caused His parents. Surely Jesus must know that He has sidetracked them and is now the reason that they are several days behind on whatever plans they had. You would expect that Jesus would be excited to see them at least, because after all, it has been a few days since He last saw them. But this is not the case at all.

Jesus does not even address the situation at hand. Jesus does not talk about why He did not make it to the family group when they left. Jesus does not address where He's been the last few days. Jesus does not even sound like He's the least bit concerned as to where His parents have been the last couple of days and why they have not been connected. And the worst part about it all is this: Jesus does not even apologize for what has happened!

There is something here that we absolutely cannot afford to miss. For as bad as this may seem, let's be clear about one thing: Jesus is unapologetic about what is happening. His parents have searched high and low for Him. His parents have had to abandon their plans to return and find their Son. And after finally discovering where Jesus is after three days... He is not even sorry? That's right, He's not sorry. In fact, He turns it around onto Mary when she questions Him and, once again, says, "Why have you been searching for Me? Didn't you know that I must be about My Father's business?"

Jesus is unapologetic about His desire and relentlessness to be about the Father's business. If you only get one thing out of this section, please get this: God is looking to raise up an *unapologetic people*. The Father is looking to raise up a people in the earth that would not be sorry about what it is that He has asked them to do. The Father is longing for the day when you would stop shying away from being about the His business because some people around you don't agree with what it is that He has asked you to do. The Father is waiting for the day when you realize that others may seem inconvenienced by what it is that God is doing in your life...but you have got to do it anyway! God is burning and patiently waits for the moment that you stand up out of all of your excuses as to why it has not been the right time for you to be about the Father's business and begin to run with what it is that He has put into your heart.

It is time to stop making excuses. It is time to realize that not everybody is going to agree. It is time to understand that maybe even some who are closest to you are not going to be able to see it at first, and may never see it. It is time to stop depending on the cheerleaders on the sideline of your life to root for you and cheer you on. It is time to wake up to the reality that God is waiting on you to be about His business.

It is time to wake up to the reality that God is waiting on you to be about His business.

Jesus' response to His parents absolutely floors me when I read over it. He does not seem to take on any of the blame that is being applied to Him. He does not make any excuses about why He feels the Father has spoken to Him about this. He simply places the responsibility back on those who should have been able to discern who He was and what it is that His life was about. Who are you? What is your life about? Do those around you know that you are completely sold out to being about the Father's business? Do those around you know that whenever they come looking for you they will find you doing the will of the Father? If not, it is time to wake up!

It was the grace of God on Jesus that empowered Him to resign Himself to the Father's business. You cannot be wholeheartedly about the Father's business and your business at the same time. You cannot say that you are all about the Father's business when you are really attempting to use the Father's business to build you own business. Many are all about their own business and continually ask the Father to follow them and bless them. I pray that this does not describe you...and if it does, you still have time to alter your course. Right now you can resign from your own way and decide once and for all that for the rest of your days you are going to, like Jesus declared to His parents, be about the Father's business!

You cannot say that you are all about the Father's business when you are really attempting to use the Father's business to build you own business.

The Apostle Paul

The apostle Paul was a man very familiar with the attempt to work out his own agenda, even in the name of serving God. Paul was passionate about what he thought was the Father's business in his day. Paul was a zealot for persecuting Christians and having them thrown in jail. Essentially, Paul would have been considered a terrorist. Paul was doing everything he knew to do in order to do what he thought was the will of God. Paul was very much alive to himself. Paul had developed a stellar résumé and a name for himself that was second to none, well, except that of the name of Jesus, whom he would soon have an encounter with. There's something about an encounter with Jesus that causes us to realize that there is only one name worth living for. There is something special about an encounter with Jesus that has the ability to ruin us for self-promotion. Paul's world would soon be rocked, and truthfully, he never saw it coming.

Paul was a man that was ruined by an encounter with Jesus. Paul had an encounter with Jesus so powerful that he was dead to himself for the rest of his days on the earth. Paul penned words like, "But whatever things were gain to me, those things I have counted as loss for the sake of Christ. More than that, I count all things to be loss in view of the surpassing value of knowing Christ Jesus my Lord, for whom I have suffered the loss of all things, and count them but rubbish so that I may gain Christ...."[106] These are the words of a man that had truly abandoned himself and his own agenda to be filled with God. Paul couldn't, nor did he want to, talk about anything else for the rest of his life.

---

[106] Phil. 3:7-8, NASB

We need more men and women like Paul who have encountered Jesus in such a real way that they have been left ruined for the things of this world and its persuasions. The world that we are living in is desperately searching and waiting for men and women to be revealed that, like Jesus, is truly about the Father's business. Paul had abandoned his own way and the pursuit of himself for a much greater pursuit, that being the pursuit of Jesus!

David

In speaking about losing our own agenda and truly being about the Father's business, I think there is a very clear example of this in the Old Testament that can easily be overlooked if we read through too quickly. The example that I would like to point to begins in verse 1 of 1 Samuel chapter 18. The story found here is describing a relationship between two men: Jonathan, the son of Saul, who is the current King of Israel; and David, the man who has been anointed by God through the prophet Samuel to one day take his place on the throne. Beginning in verse 1 it says, "As soon as he had finished speaking to Saul, the soul of Jonathan was knit to David, and Jonathan loved him as his own soul."[107]

---

[107] 1 Sam. 18:1, ESV

I find it to be very interesting the way that God works at times in our lives, especially after viewing this situation with David. David is carrying a word from God that he is supposed to one day step into the position that Jonathan's dad is currently occupying. Yet, even though David is anointed to be the next king of Israel, God does not just walk him into the palace so that he can take over. God first walks David into a relationship with the king's son, Jonathan; interesting. And this is not just some ordinary relationship. David and Jonathan were very close; the best of friends; brothers.

> **The world that we are living in is desperately searching and waiting for men and women to be revealed that, like Jesus, is truly about the Father's business.**

A few verses later we find, "Then Jonathan made a covenant with David, because he loved him as his own soul. And Jonathan stripped himself of the robe that was on him and gave it to David, and his armor, and even his sword and his bow and belt."[108] Jonathan loved David. Jonathan loved David as his own soul; that is deep. This is not something superficial; this is for real. It is a very peculiar thing for God to give

---

[108] 1 Sam. 18:3-4, ESV

David a covenant brother in Jonathan. Why would I say that? I don't find it to be odd that God would give David a covenant brother. The "who" is not the issue; we should all have covenant relationships. However, I do find God's selection of Jonathan interesting.

As you read through the story in 1 Samuel you will see clearly that Jonathan looked out for David in times that he desperately needed it, and also helped to save his life on occasion when his dad, Saul, was ready to kill him. Yet, even with all that is happening on the surface, there is something happening beneath the surface that we can't miss. There is something happening here in the heart of David that we must talk about. For as much as the Scriptures reveal to us about the relationship between David and Jonathan, David passes a very important test that we too will confront.

There are a few things to note about this story quickly before we continue: David was anointed to be king. Jonathan's father was currently king. Jonathan should have had a better chance, being the king's son, of getting into the throne. Got it? Okay, let's continue.

This relationship with Jonathan is something that could have been very advantageous for David. I mean, clearly God was setting him up on the inside track in giving him Jonathan as a covenant brother. Jonathan would have been willing to do anything for David. Surely David could clearly see that God was setting him up with this relationship to move him closer to what it is that He had spoken over him and set in his sights for the future. Jonathan would be David's bridge into the palace and onto the throne. Right? Wrong. And not just wrong, but very wrong.

Never once is it recorded that David attempts to leverage his relationship with Jonathan in order to work himself into the fulfillment of all that God had spoken to him. Never once do we see David trying to walk his way across the bridge of relationship in order to better position himself for his destiny. You will not find a moment where David pulls Jonathan aside and leverages the covenant that he and Jonathan had entered into in order for a quicker outcome to be achieved with his promised kingship. David just does not do it. Why does any of this matter? I am really glad that you asked.

If I have realized anything in my time walking with God it is this: God will at times test us with the relationships that he gives us.

David is unwilling to maneuver his way into the promise of God by manipulating a relationship that God had clearly given him with Jonathan. If I have realized anything in my time walking with God it is this: God will at times test us with the relationships that he gives us. God will allow you to enter into relationships, and some of those relationships will be very close, covenant relationships even, with those who are living the outcome that you desire. God will let you get really close to those who have what it is that you want, what it is that He has promised you, in order to see what will come out of you, how you will handle the test. David's relationship with Jonathan was a test for the heart of David.

David sees something on the inside that he cannot yet seize on the outside. David's test is not one of validity; it is one of integrity. What David sees on the inside is valid; it is from God. God surely anointed him to be the next king of Israel. God did give him a great promise of what his future would look like. None of this is the issue. The issue lies in, what will David do about what he knows God has said? The question is not whether or not David will get there as much as it is, how will he choose to get there? This is what God waits to see. The way that David chooses to handle the promise of God in his life is the great revealer of where David's dependency lies; will he choose to trust God and wait for Him?

David proved faithful because he chose to trust God. David was found trustworthy because he was not willing to manipulate the system in order to gain a sooner outcome. David chose the higher road, which is to trust the Father to fulfill His business in his life. Jonathan was indeed a covenant brother, and David did not allow that to become polluted by his own selfish interests and agenda.

Are you jealous for the purity of your relationships? Your relationships are not just in place to serve you. Your relationships are not there for you to massage them into what can be a great benefit to you. Do you really trust God enough to fulfill His business through your life? A clear way to examine the truth of your statements is to evaluate the way you treat those, and view those, who are living the outcome that you know God has clearly spoken to you about.

Can you identify any way that God is testing you by the relationships that He has given you? Are you passing those tests?

Selfish agendas are dangerous. Selfish agendas are a cancerous substance that have the potential to put to death even the best of relationships when revealed. Can you identify any way that God is testing you by the relationships that He has given you? Are you passing those tests? If not, you can right now make the choice to surrender your own agenda and trust the Father. David proved faithful. Jesus proved faithful. It is possible for you to also prove yourself faithful.

Please take a few moments to watch my video as I
encourage you with what it means to learn:

"The Rhythm of the Spirit"

https://vimeo.com/122181498

9

Laid-Down Lovers

———⊶∞∞⊷———

"The opportunity of a lifetime must be seized within the lifetime of the opportunity."

—Leonard Ravenhill[109]

Every generation God looks for a man or a woman that He can use to impact that generation. Every generation God seeks for an access point, a point of penetration. Every generation God seeks out a breaking point! God is constantly trying to break into a generation, constantly yearning for the moment when a man or woman would answer the knocking on the door of the heart and allow Him in.

---

[109] "Leonard Ravenhill's Ministry Quotes, "http://www.leonard-ravenhill.com/quotes.

You can search back through the history of the ages and move from man to man, woman to woman, and identify those who have received empowerment from God to lay their lives down and shape the generation of which they were placed to live. Again, consider with me for a moment: In all of the history of the world, you have been hand selected to be alive during these days...right here...right now. God chose you to be a part of all that is happening in the world right now. Rather than making excuses about why your life will never matter and how God will never use you to do anything significant, realize that you are alive for such a time as this and rise to the challenge of the day. Rise to the call of God on your life and watch Him work wonders through your surrender to being about His business.

Rise to the call of God on your life and watch Him work wonders through your surrender to being about His business.

God has always been able to find His man or woman. Let's take a look at some of those that have resigned themselves to the Father's business and have been used to make a mark on their generation. There are countless lives throughout history that we could turn to, but I want to examine a few key individuals found in the Scriptures that I have been praying would arise once again in our day. Those namely being: David, Jonah, and John the Baptist.

David

First Samuel chapter 16 brings David into God's story unfolding throughout the Old Testament of the Bible. David is a young boy and is out herding sheep when the prophet Samuel shows up to his house with a word from God that he has arrived to anoint the next king of Israel. David is the last one invited to the party because his father and the rest of his brothers overlook him.[110] However, though he was last on man's list, he was first on God's.

God speaks to Samuel that he is to anoint David to be the next king of Israel before all those that are in attendance that day. What a way to get brought into the story! It would appear that David does not seem to fit the model of what Israel had hoped for in a king to lead them, but again, God seems to have a different vantage point of who we are than those that surround us. God sees things very differently than we do when we are performing our evaluations of people's worthiness or readiness. Though David did not seem to have the favor of people going for him, he had the favor of God upon his life, and that is all that mattered.

---

[110] 1 Sam. 16:3-10, NIV

Let's fast-forward into a later portion of David's life. In the next chapter of 1 Samuel we find that the children of Israel are in somewhat of a battle with the Philistines. I say somewhat because the Bible does not actually mention that anyone engaged in any physical combat up until this point. The Philistines were encamped in Ephes-dammim, which was between Socoh and Azekah. The Israelites were gathered together and encamped in the Valley of Elah. The Philistines stood on a mountain on one side, and Israel stood on a mountain on the other side, with a valley between them.[111]

I can definitely understand why no one seemed to be chomping at the bit to engage the Philistines' giant-sized champion in the valley of opportunity.

The Philistine champion Goliath, who was a giant of a man, came out day by day for forty days and taunted the children of Israel. Goliath attempted to provoke the army of Israel to come out and fight him, and if somehow victorious against him, the Philistines would surrender to Israel and become their slaves. For some reason, there was no one from Israel's side who seemed to be up for the challenge. After all, according to the

---

[111] 1 Sam. 17:1-3, NASB

description, Goliath is said to have been over nine feet tall![112] I can definitely understand why no one seemed to be chomping at the bit to engage the Philistines' giant-sized champion in the valley of opportunity.

While all of this is happening, David enters back into the story. Some time has passed now and David has been back out in the field tending to the sheep. David's father makes a call for David to go down to the battle lines to check in on his brothers to see how they are doing and also to take them some supplies from their father.[113] When David arrives, the Israelites are in the Valley of Elah fighting with the Philistines.

Something quite interesting happens on the day that David arrives to the front line of battle that had not happened up until that point. David finds his way down to the front lines, not because he had a desire to get into a fight and show off his skills, but because he is being sent with the task of bringing assistance to some that are currently engaged in the battle. When David arrives he sees the same thing that has been happening for the past forty days. What is that, you ask? I am glad you would like to know.

For forty days, the Bible says, the children of Israel came out and stood before the Philistines. For forty days the children of Israel heard the taunting of the

---

[112] 1 Sam. 17:4, NASB

[113] 1 Sam. 17:17-18, NIV

giant morning and night. For forty days the children of Israel, when posed with the opportunity to get involved in the fight against the Philistines, decided to retreat and give in to their fears. The Bible says that day by day when they heard the words of the Philistine giant they were dismayed and greatly afraid.[114]

For forty days the children of Israel, when posed with the opportunity to get involved in the fight against the Philistines, decided to retreat and give in to their fears.

Please consider for just a moment that this was not just a ragtag bunch of individuals that were gathered at the Valley of Elah. This was not the B Team that Israel had put on the field; this was the best that Israel had to offer. They had on the right battle gear, the correct dress for the occasion. They knew the right battle formations, and would line themselves up accordingly. They even knew the right battle chants. So, let's see, the right dress, the right formations, and the right chants. However, even equipped with all of this it did not seem to make a difference in the fight that stood before them.

This is where David finds himself, on the front lines with the leading warriors of the day who are scared to

---

[114] 1 Sam. 17:11, NIV

death and refuse to enter into the valley of opportunity where the giant stands. David does not have the right dress. David does not know the proper formations. David is not trained in the chants that are required for the moment. But, that day, out on the front lines, when the giant set himself up and began to taunt once again, after forty days of successful intimidation executed against the children of Israel, the Bible interjects a difference maker into the unfolding story. The Bible says on that day the Philistine came out and spoke to them according to the same words…and *David heard*!

That day in the valley of opportunity the Bible tells us that David heard the words of the giant. That day David heard the taunting of the Philistine champion. That day, although seeming to be there for a different purpose, David's ears were opened to the voice of the enemy in his generation.

To move through the rest of the details rather quickly, I will sum it up with this: David hears, David responds, David trusts God, David triumphs! That day David heard the enemy, yet he had a very different response than what the rest of the warriors of his day were offering. David not only responds, but David actually ends up in the valley running full speed toward the very thing that everyone else was running from. Hear this again, David runs towards the thing everyone else is running from!

David not only stands his ground against the enemy; David overtakes the enemy and occupies the ground that the enemy believed to be sure-footed upon.[115] David is used to bring one of the greatest victories to Israel throughout all of their history; David makes a mark on his generation by coming off the sidelines and getting into the game. David steps up for God and God steps up in David in a bigger way than the giant that stood before him.

How is any of this possible? Once again, I am glad you asked. David enters into a place of service, and through serving, his ears are opened to the taunting of the enemy. Through serving, God allows David to become aware of what the voice of the enemy in his day sounds like. David did not go chasing after the enemy. David was chasing after God, and by doing so, God entrusted to David the opportunity to overtake the enemy.

I love these words: and David heard. Have you heard? Have you identified what the voice of the enemy sounds like in your generation? Do you know what the taunts of Goliath are saying to the church in the day that you have been chosen to live? Are you familiar with the ground that the enemy is occupying? These are very important questions to consider.

---

[115] 1 Sam. 17:48-51, NIV

David heard! The children of Israel had all of the right external things in place: right dress, right formations, and right chants, yet did not have the right response. David did not have any of the right external things going for him, yet he heard and had the response that God was waiting for! Don't underestimate what God could do, and would do, with your life once your ears have been opened.

Don't underestimate what God could do, and would do, with your life once your ears have been opened.

Maybe you have been told that you don't have any of the right things going for you. Maybe you have been told that you don't have the right dress. Maybe you don't have the right training. Maybe you don't have the right formations. Your entire life will change when you realize that God is not looking for the same thing that man is requiring of you. God is not so much concerned with whether or not you have the greatest gifting. God is not so much concerned about whether or not you have been through the best schooling. God is not even so much worried about whether or not you have been brought up in the best of training. God is looking for a man or woman that is available.

Are you available? Are you willing to serve? Are you willing to have your ears opened to the voice of the enemy in your generation? Are you willing to stand for God and have God stand taller in you than the giants of your day? If so, I pray that today you would hear the voice of the Holy Spirit crying out: I am looking for someone who is available!

Don't simply give your life to lesser things because you are intimidated and very afraid because of the size of the giant and the violence of his taunting. God is able!

David ran toward what everyone else was running from. One day we will all stand before God and give an account for what we have done with the life that we were given. We will stand before God and answer for our works that were done here and now in the flesh.[116] God has gone to great lengths to invest in you, and there will be a day when the Master evaluates the return on that investment.[117] Let us on that day be able to say with great confidence that we did not run from Goliath. Let us be able to answer for our lives that we gave everything of what was invested to us to take on the giants in our generation. Don't simply give your life to lesser things because you are intimidated and very afraid because of the size of the giant and the violence of his taunting. God is able!

---

[116] 2 Cor. 5:10, NIV
[117] Matt. 25:19, NASB

I pray that Davids would arise in our day. I pray Davids' ears would be opened to hear. I pray for the obedience of Davids to begin to run toward the thing that the church is equipped for yet won't face. I pray for the humility of David to realize that this fight is about God and not them. Thank You, Father, for Davids!

God is waiting to break into a generation through the life of Davids!

Jonah

Jonah chapter 1 brings us the person of Jonah into God's unfolding story; Jonah is a prophet. The book opens by telling us that the word of the Lord comes to Jonah saying, "Arise, go to Nineveh, that great city, and cry out against it; for their wickedness has come up before Me."[118] Now, you would think that because he is a prophet that he would be quick to jump up from whatever it is that he had going on to invest himself into the obedience of the word that he knows has just come to him from the Lord. However, the Bible actually tells us something a little different. In the next verse we learn, "But Jonah arose to flee to Tarshish from the presence of the LORD. He went down to Joppa, and found a ship going to Tarshish;

---

[118] Jonah 1:1-2, NKJV

so he paid the fare and went down into it, to go with them to Tarshish from the presence of the LORD."[119]

This does not seem like the proper response that you would expect from a prophet. This can't be the way that a true prophet would respond to the word of the Lord in his life. Yet, even with all of what we would want to believe about a prophet, Jonah is running the opposite direction from where it is that God has told him to go. Jonah is full speed ahead in disobedience. Before we fault Jonah for his behavior, let's examine his situation a little further to see if we can find out what would warrant this type of response from someone who clearly walked with God and was able to hear His voice when He spoke to him.

What was it that was being asked of Jonah that he was running from? God asked Jonah to arise and go to Nineveh. Nineveh was the capital city of Assyria, which is modern-day Iraq. In Jonah's day the Assyrians were some of the wickedest people on the face of the earth. The Assyrians were known for the way they ruthlessly and unashamedly killed people and used brutal tactics to overthrow cities. The Assyrians were also the people that were known for plaguing the Israelites. The Assyrians were definitely not friendly, and they were not nice about the way they went about

---

[119] Jonah 1:3, NKJV

implementing their strategy of dominating those around them.

Jonah obviously was not excited about this assignment from God for his life. The Assyrians would not have been the first people group on your list that you would schedule if you were trying to put together preaching opportunities. The Assyrians, actually, would not have made the list at all. There were countless reasons that I am sure Jonah had as to why he did not want to go and preach to them. Yet, even with all of the reasons that Jonah could have presented as a "Why Not," God was trying to get a hold of a man to send him their way.

Even with all of what we would want to believe about a prophet, Jonah is running the opposite direction from where it is that God has told him to go.

The Bible tells us that Jonah runs in the opposite direction of where God was asking him to go. Not only did he go the opposite way, he paid to board a ship to get as far away as he could. I don't want to belabor the point that Jonah did not want to do what was being asked of him, but it plays a crucial part in the point that we are building here. Jonah was not excited about what God said to him and he did not want to do it.

Jonah is now a man on the run. While he is on the run he ends up boarding a ship. While at sea the Lord sent a great wind on the sea that was about to rip the boat to shreds. The other passengers were afraid for their lives and thought they were about to die because the conditions had gotten so rough. They all began to throw their cargo off of the boat thinking that this would be a solution.[120]

Finally someone went downstairs to find Jonah, who was sleeping in the lowest part of the boat and woke him up in order for him to call on the name of his God so that they would not perish.[121] They knew that Jonah was a Hebrew and that he feared the Lord because he had told them. Let's fast-forward a little bit. After going back and forth with Jonah, the men decide they are going to throw Jonah overboard into the waters. This is where the well-known story of Jonah comes from. When Jonah is thrown over, the Lord prepared a great fish to swallow Jonah, and Jonah was in the belly of the fish three days and three nights.[122]

Chapter 2 of Jonah gives us a little bit of an insider's view as to what is happening in Jonah's heart as all of this crazy stuff is happening to him. He's been running from God's assignment for his life. He found himself

---

[120] Jonah 1:5, NKJV
[121] Jonah 1:6, NKJV
[122] Jonah 1:15-17, NKJV

on a ship heading in the opposite direction of where God said to go. He ended up getting himself thrown overboard by the other passengers on that boat attempting to save their own lives. After being thrown overboard he is swallowed by a great fish. It is at this point in Jonah's life that he remembers the Lord. It is at this point in Jonah's life that his eyes turn upward toward God. In the belly of that great fish Jonah decides to pray.

It is at this point in Jonah's life that his eyes turn upward toward God. In the belly of that great fish Jonah decides to pray.

When it seems as if Jonah is at his lowest of lows, the Bible gives us a sentence that changes the game for Jonah in the beginning of chapter 3: Now the word of the LORD came to Jonah a second time, saying, "Arise, go to Nineveh, that great city, and preach to it the message that I tell you."[123] The same word that Jonah had received at an earlier point in his life has now returned to him. Now standing before Jonah is another opportunity to fulfill God's assignment for his life.

This time Jonah has a very different response than the first time. Verse 3 tells us, "So Jonah arose and

---

[123] Jonah 3:1-2, NKJV

went to Nineveh, according to the word of the LORD.[124] God finally had Jonah's obedience. Jonah went into Nineveh and declared that after forty days God would overthrow the city because of their wickedness.[125] At the preaching of Jonah the Bible says that the people of Nineveh believed God, proclaimed a fast, and put on sackcloth from the greatest to the least of them. Even the king of Nineveh himself arose from his throne and laid aside his robe, covered himself with sackcloth, and sat in ashes.[126] When Nineveh responded in this fashion, the Bible tells us that God saw their works and relented from the disaster that He said He would bring upon them, and He did not do it.[127]

The city of Nineveh's repentance and salvation from God hinged upon the obedience of Jonah doing what God asked him to do. Really? All of those lives hinged upon the obedience of one man fulfilling what God was asking him to do? Could not God have just risen up someone else or spoken to someone else about going to Nineveh if Jonah really did not want to go? It would be easy to get wrapped up in that debate and miss the simplicity of what the Scriptures are illustrating to us, and that is this: Jonah was not

---

[124] Jonah 3:3, NKJV
[125] Jonah 3:4, NKJV
[126] Jonah 3:5-6, NKJV
[127] Jonah 3:10, NKJV

forgotten about even though he did not respond right the first time.

God pursued Jonah. In amazing mercy God allowed Jonah to run and do his own thing for a little while. In great love God patiently sat by and watched as Jonah decided that he had better plans than what it was God was trying to accomplish. Jonah ran; God waited. How long would God have waited? Surely there must come a point when God decides that if Jonah is not going to respond in obedience that He is going to have to recruit someone else to get the job done. Again, this is not the place for that debate. All that we have here in the book of Jonah lets us know that God waited, and not only waited, but the word of the Lord came a second time to Jonah!

In great love God patiently sat by and watched as Jonah decided that he had better plans than what it was God was trying to accomplish.

Do you find yourself in a similar situation like Jonah did? Do you know that God has spoken something to you that you really don't want to do? Are you aware of a word of the Lord that has come to you about going to a people and preaching to them? Are there people in our day that you feel, like Jonah, you would rather not go and preach to? Are there other things you could imagine yourself doing? If so, I pray that the word of the Lord would come to you a second time.

There are cities that depend on your obedience. There are states that depend on your obedience. There are nations and peoples that depend on your obedience. The word that God has given to you is the hinge point for deliverance and salvation. Your obedience to what God is saying could mean revival for a wicked and sinful people, even as it did in Jonah's days of preaching to Nineveh.

> **The word that God has given to you is the hinge point for deliverance and salvation. Your obedience to what God is saying could mean revival for a wicked and sinful people.**

I pray that right now you would have a moment of sobriety. I pray that right now your eyes and ears would be opened to the reality and weight of the call of God upon your life. I pray that you would once and for all realize that while you are running, God is waiting, and people are waiting for you to fulfill the word of the Lord in your life. I pray for Jonahs to arise in our day! I pray for the obedience of Jonahs around the world, in Jesus' name. Amen!

God is waiting to break into a generation through the life of Jonahs!

John the Baptist

There is one more individual that I would like to highlight as we continue our journey together, and that individual is John the Baptist. Matthew presents us with his introduction of John in the third chapter of his gospel. John is out in the wilderness preaching and saying, "Repent, for the kingdom of heaven is at hand!"[128] Matthew is also quick to make sure the reference about John is known to all that he is the one of whom Isaiah prophesied about saying, "The voice of one crying in the wilderness: Prepare the way of the LORD; Make His paths straight."[129]

Matthew gives us a good visual of what type of dress and diet John kept: he was clothed in camel's hair, with a leather belt around his waist; and his food was locusts and wild honey.[130] John must have been an interesting guy, for sure. John would have been interesting, but he was not this way by accident. In fact, John was this way by divine design. John's birth is one that was foretold to his parents by an angelic encounter that Luke gives us insight to in the writing of his gospel.

---

128 Matt. 3:2, NKJV
129 Matt. 3:3, NKJV
130 Matt. 3:4, NKJV

Luke chapter 1 tells us that Gabriel, an angel of the Lord, came to John's father, Zacharias, in response to him crying out in prayer about having a child. Gabriel tells Zacharias some pretty incredible things about John and the purpose that God has for his life. Gabriel says,

> "Do not be afraid, Zacharias, for your prayer is heard; and your wife Elizabeth will bear you a son, and you shall call his name John. And you will have joy and gladness, and many will rejoice at his birth. For he will be great in the sight of the Lord, and shall drink neither wine nor strong drink. He will also be filled with the Holy Spirit, even from his mother's womb. And he will turn many of the children of Israel to the Lord their God. He will also go before Him in the spirit and power of Elijah, 'to turn the hearts of the fathers to the children,' and the disobedient to the wisdom of the just, to make ready a people prepared for the Lord."[131]

What an amazing setup for John! We are not talking about some little task. John sounds like he has an enormous amount of responsibility laid upon his life before he is ever even conceived. John is the one

---

[131] Luke 1:13-17, NKJV

that Gabriel tells of that will turn many of the children of Israel to the Lord their God. John is the one who will prepare the way for Jesus to make His entrance.

With this type of extraordinary presentation given to John's dad, you could probably imagine that God would have a beautiful way to lead John into preparation for the magnitude of what his life will mean; and yes, God did have a great way to prepare John. God sent him into the wilderness for many years. John sat out in the wilderness and spent time with God.

How can this be the best way that God saw fit to prepare John for all that He had for him in life? Wouldn't it have made more sense for John to go to the best ministry schools of his day? I mean, after all, God was going to use him as a voice to turn the hearts of many back to the Lord their God. Wouldn't John have to have the most recognized credentials attached to his business card and website in order for men to receive his message well? Surely no one would come and listen to John if he could not verify his covering, his status, and his title.

Even going against what would seem like the popular wisdom of the day, the next verse of Matthew's gospel gives us a pretty phenomenal piece of information. Matthew says this, "Then, Jerusalem, all Judea, and all the region around the Jordan went out to him and were baptized by him in the Jordan, confessing their sins."[132] Please read that one more time. Jerusalem, *all* Judea, and *all* the region around the Jordan went out to him. John had people coming, looking for him.

John was drawing *all* of the people from the region to the wilderness. Or better put this way: Because John went after God, God brought people after John. John was in the right place at the right time, and because of that, God rallied people around John to hear what he was crying out. All of the people from the region were seeking after the one whom God had sent out into the wilderness.

John's cry was developed in the wilderness. The substance of what John had to say was refined in isolation. John's message wasn't copied from the most polished preachers of his day. John was raw; John was real; John was resigned to God and obedience to God alone. It is because of this that God was able to trust John with all of the region. I continue to use the word "all" in the description of John's effectiveness because I want you to realize that the Scriptures are telling us "all" for a reason! This was not just a percentage; this was all! God entrusted John with astounding influence.

When John's cry was ready, God brought the people to hear it. God did not bring people because of

---

[132] Matt. 3:5-6, NKJV

John's Facebook following. God did not bring people because of how many followers he had on Twitter, or how many likes his last Instagram post acquired. It was not because John had a brilliant marketing strategy to draw people to the wilderness. It was not because John's website was breathtaking. All John had was a cry, and that cry was all God was looking for!

> **John entrusted himself to God's influence, and God entrusted people to John's influence.**

John was tucked away in obscurity waiting for the day that the activation button would be pressed in his life. John was fully given over to God. I am sure that John had a sense that God would use him, or that God had a special purpose for his life. I am sure that his parents told him about the events that surrounded his birth and encouraged him that God had a great plan for him. I am sure that John would remind God of all the things that he said about Him in his time of waiting and preparation. And when the day finally came, the same John that had been crying out in private was now crying out in public!

I absolutely love this! John entrusted himself to God's influence, and God entrusted people to John's influence. You may be reading through this and asking yourself, "What does this have anything to do with me?" I am really glad that you asked, because this has everything to do with you.

Do you find yourself in a place of obscurity? Do you find yourself carrying a great sense of purpose yet not really knowing how to do anything with what you sense? Do you feel as if all you have been able to do is cry out to God about things that have "yet to be" in your life that you know He has spoken to you or shown you? If you answered yes to any of these questions, this has everything to do with you.

Maybe you find yourself in a place much like John did, alone with God in an isolated place. This doesn't necessarily mean that you have been isolated from people; you don't have to be isolated from people in order to still feel as if you have been in a backwoods place according to God's purpose for your life. If you feel as if you have not yet been able to connect with what it is that God has said to you, I want to encourage you with this: develop your cry.

Don't give yourself over to how you are going to build your influence; build up your cry. Don't constantly worry about how God is going to get you in a public place so that people can hear what you know has been burning in your heart; stay faithful to cry out in the private place and let God handle the rest. Allow God to develop the substance of your cry in hiddenness, and when ready, those things that have been hidden, God will reveal to all the region!

If you feel like all you have is a cry, you are in the right place. Let God develop the cry that will draw regions to you. Once your cry is developed you won't have to go chasing people; God will bring people to you. When your cry is developed you won't have to attempt to build your own platform. The place where you stand, even if it is out in the wilderness, will be the place that God causes the regions to come to. Sometimes God will send you to the regions, but in John's case, the regions came to him, and it was God's doing.

Allow God to develop the substance of your cry in hiddenness, and when ready, those things that have been hidden, God will reveal to all the region!

Don't allow your time of hiddenness to go to waste because you can't see the visible effects of God taking you aside to Himself. You have to trust that God is faithful, and that He is more jealous to fulfill those things He has spoken to you than you are excited to see them unfold in your own life. God is waiting for your cry to be fully developed. God is waiting for the thing that He has burning on the inside of you to come to full flame in order to allow it to be released at large.

I think it is also important to mention here that we can't judge influence by the size of a crowd. Sure, there are many who will have influence with nations, some with regions, and others with cities. However, our lives are no less significant if our influence lies within our school campus. Our lives do not have less meaning because our influence is set aside for our workplace. Your greatest

God is waiting for the thing that He has burning on the inside of you to come to full flame in order to allow it to be released at large.

influence can be within your home, and in fact, I will tell you that is the place where you must always begin. Do not think that God will give you influence outside if you don't first desire to have influence inside. Don't underestimate what God is doing in your life because you are trying to quantify it.

There is a day coming when God will hit the activate button in your life! I am praying that God would hit the activate button in the lives of Johns all over the world. I am praying for those that have given themselves to the wilderness places of life and have tucked themselves away to be with God in order to develop their cry. I am praying for the substance of your cry to be fully refined. I am praying for the voices that only God has heard up until this point in obscurity to be released to the regions, cities, and tribes of this world! The world is waiting for you, John!

God is waiting to break into a generation through the life of Johns!

Please take a few moments to watch this short
stirring video from one of today's most prominent
and powerful voices:

"Laid-Down Lovers for Jesus"

https://vimeo.com/122181581

10

Do Something About It!

———⊶⊷———

"We can be in our day what the heroes of faith were in their day—but remember at the time they didn't know they were heroes."

—A. W. Tozer[133]

I t is incredible to reflect into the lives of men and women that have heard from God and at some point in their life decided to do something about it. This thought provokes me to ask you some questions: What are you doing with what it is that God has spoken to you? What are you doing with the words of Jesus in your life? Have you actually stepped into what it is that you know is being spoken, or has been

[133] "Popular Quotes," A. W. Tozer, goodreads, www.goodreads.com.

spoken, to you? It is not enough just to know what God is saying to us; we actually have to get up and do something about it.

In Matthew chapter 10 Jesus makes a statement that many easily read over because as believers we feel that it would not apply to us because of our confession of faith. Jesus says these words to those listening that day, and to us today, "Whoever acknowledges me before others, I will also acknowledge before my Father in heaven. But whoever disowns me before others, I will disown before my Father in heaven."[134] These seem to be very strong words, and the point that Jesus is making comes across loud and clear. But what does it actually mean to disown Jesus before others? What would it look like for someone to really be unwilling to acknowledge Jesus before others? Before we quickly read over these words and think that they do not apply to us, I believe it would help if we answer these questions.

We cannot simply go on living our life thinking that what Jesus is talking about in these verses found in Matthew chapter 10 is a mental ascent of His existence. Many, if asked if they believe in Jesus, would have no problem answering with a decisive yes. But is that all it means to acknowledge Jesus before others? Is the only

---

[134] Matt. 10:32-33, NIV

thing that Jesus is looking for a cute little theological agreement of His existence? Do we really believe that it is enough just to check off Christian on our religious preference questionnaire? I don't think so. Why would I say such a thing? I say such a thing for this reason: even the devil believes in Jesus. As you journey through the Gospels you will find that demons had a greater recognition of who Jesus was most times more than the crowds that surrounded Him in a given setting.[135] We cannot be lured into believing that what Jesus means here is just a little head nod in the right direction about who He is; there is more.

How could I be one that acknowledges Jesus before others if just saying that I believe in Him is not enough?

How could I be one that acknowledges Jesus before others if just saying that I believe in Him is not enough? What would I have to do? Now we are on the right track, I believe there is something that Jesus actually wants us to do in order to acknowledge Him before others. In Matthew chapter 7 Jesus is found issuing these words, "Therefore anyone who hears these words of mine and puts them into practice is like a wise man who built his house on the rock."[136] Let me

---

[135] Matt. 8:29, NIV
[136] Matt. 7:24, NIV

emphasize a portion of this for us: anyone who hears these words of mine and *puts them into practice*. Another translation says it this way, "Therefore everyone who hears these words of Mine and *acts on them*...."[137]

We need to realize that Jesus is looking for a people that are willing to act on what it is that He is saying; He is desirous of a people that are passionate about putting His words into practice. It is not enough to simply know what it is that Jesus is saying. There must be a corresponding *doing* to what He is saying. There were many that knew Jesus' words, yet weren't willing to actually step into what it was that He was saying. Herein lies the issue of acknowledgement; it is an issue of hearing and doing.

It is vital for us as we follow Jesus that we do not sidestep the issue of His words. In fact, His words have always been an issue. You cannot love the man, Christ Jesus, without loving what it is that He is saying; the two are inseparable. The words reveal the heart of the man. Jesus Himself said it this way, "For out of the abundance of the heart the mouth speaks."[138] The words that He is speaking reveal what is bound up in His heart, and this cannot be a side issue; it must become central to us. In speaking to you Jesus is

---

[137] Matt. 7:24, NASB (emphasis mine)
[138] Matt. 12:34, ESV

entrusting you with His heart, because again, the heart is revealed in the words.

You cannot pick and choose what things you like about all that Jesus had to say and decide that you will not make the other things a priority. We must choose to love Him in His entirety, and that means loving all of what it is that He has said. We also cannot choose to come up with our own interpretation in order to make what Jesus has said more palatable. An unwillingness to change will cause many to want to redefine what Jesus has said in order to reconcile a way to continue walking with Him. This must not be.

We must choose to love Him in His entirety, and that means loving all of what it is that He has said.

The issue has always been, and will always be, what Jesus had to say. In John chapter 6 the crowd that surrounded Jesus on that day was okay walking with Him until He began to say certain things. Jesus tells them, "I am the bread of life. Whoever comes to me will never go hungry, and whoever believes in me will never be thirsty."[139] To this the Jews there began to grumble about Him *because He said*....[140] Jesus then says, "I am the living bread that came down from

---

[139] John 6:35, NIV
[140] John 6:41, NIV (emphasis mine)

heaven. Whoever eats this bread will live forever. This bread is my flesh, which I will give for the life of the world." Again, then the Jews began to argue sharply among themselves, *because of what he said*....[141] And the issue at hand surfaces in verse 60, "On hearing what he said, many of his disciples said, 'This is a hard teaching. Who can accept it?'"[142] And the final blow, which illustrates our point, is found in verse 66, "As a result of this many of His disciples withdrew and were not walking with Him anymore."[143] Let's rephrase this last verse this way: As a result of what Jesus was saying, many withdrew and were unwilling to walk with Him.

I find that the issue was never with what Jesus was doing; it was always with what it was that He was saying. In fact, people loved the things that He was doing. They loved the healing, the provision in the feeding of the multitudes, the cleansing of the lepers. The issue was never the miracles, or the activity; the issue was always with the words. The Jews in John chapter 10 told Jesus, "We're not stoning you for anything good you did, but for what you said—this blasphemy of calling yourself God."[144] I want you to notice a common thread here in the verses that I

---

[141] John 6:51-52, NIV (emphasis mine)
[142] John 6:60, NIV
[143] John 6:66, NASB
[144] John 10:33, MSG

have presented to you, and it is this: those who had a problem with Jesus, had a problem with what He had to say.

Do you have a problem with what Jesus is saying? Are you one that takes issue with certain statements that Jesus made, or is making? Again, we cannot love the man without loving His words. People that tell me they love Jesus, yet they don't have any concern for His words, are deceived. There is this idea that you can love Jesus and just separate Him from what the Bible reveals about Him by His words. This is an absolute atrocity and one of the greatest tricks of the enemy in the day we live. By being lovers of His words, we become lovers of the person.

I find that the issue was never with what Jesus was doing; it was always with what it was that He was saying.

Being a lover of His words doesn't mean that we just simply choose to like what He has said. We must be willing to, like Jesus said, put these words into practice. We have to be willing to do what the disciples walking with Him in John chapter 6 were unwilling to do, and that is this: accept them and step into them. There is an action that is required for acknowledgement.

Why is acting on the words of Jesus such a big deal? We must remember that Jesus is the Word made manifest. Jesus is the personification of the Word. When Jesus spoke the word, He was just speaking about Himself; He was speaking out of what He already was. John 1 tells us that the Word became flesh and dwelt among us.[145] Jesus is the Word wrapped in flesh that came to walk amongst men.

When we choose to step into the words of Jesus we ourselves are allowing the Word to once again take upon itself flesh and dwell among men; this is huge! Stepping into the words of Jesus gives opportunity for the revelation of Jesus to be made known. John the Baptist in John chapter 1 said that he was sent to baptize so that Jesus would be revealed to Israel.[146] He stepped into the words that were spoken to him, and in that place of obedience, or willingness to acknowledge by putting action to the words, Jesus was revealed to a people. Being willing to put action to the words is no small issue. The revelation of Jesus is on the line!

We must step into the words of Jesus so the revelation of Jesus can impact a generation. There must be action to the things that we ourselves have heard. James says that we must not only be hearers of the word, so to deceive ourselves, but doers.[147] Many will

---

[145] John 1:14, NASB
[146] John 1:31-33, HCSB
[147] James 1:22, HCSB

hear the word, but doing the word means everything. The difference between those that hear and those that do is action. Action means putting what we hear into practice. Jesus said this would be how we acknowledge Him before others.

The way that you will acknowledge Jesus before others is to do what He is saying to you. This can be as simple or as profound as you would like it to be, or it can be profoundly simple.

Jesus is speaking to you because He wants to be revealed in and through you. The things that He is asking you to do is leading to the revelation of who He is being made known to a people. Just like John, as we go and do what it is that we are hearing, Jesus will be revealed. Now, this is great for those that actually go and do what it is that they are hearing. But what about those that are unwilling to go and do?

Just like John, as we go and do what it is that we are hearing, Jesus will be revealed.

What would cause you to be unwilling to go and do what Jesus is saying? Are you afraid of what the outcome will be? Are you worried about what people are going to think about you? Do you in some way feel under qualified for the task of which He is asking you to give your action to? I would like for you to realize that none of these are good enough excuses to refuse to act on what you hear, and at the end of the day, even the best excuse…is still an excuse. We must take action!

I don't want to overcomplicate this, so let's simplify it this way. When you are willing to put the words of Jesus into practice, He is **If you want to be** revealed to your family. When **connected to the** you put action to what you hear, **heart of Jesus,** He is revealed to those **you have to be** surrounding you day to day in **connected to** your workplace. When you are **His words.** willing to acknowledge Him, by stepping into His words, those on your school campus get to see Jesus, by seeing the word fleshed out in your life. The revelation of Jesus comes to those who see the word in action.

Your commitment to the words of Jesus must have an expression; they must have an outlet in order for the validity of what you say to be seen. The way that this happens is by putting His words into practice. The person that obeys what Jesus is saying is the person that loves Him. Jesus has a love language, and it is obedience. Hear that again: Jesus' love language is obedience. He said Himself, "If you love me, obey my commandments."[148] His commandments are the

---

[148] John 14:15, NLT

words that He spoke, which reveal His heart. If you want to be connected to the heart of Jesus, you have to be connected to His words.

An unwillingness to put those words into practice is the place that Jesus mentioned when He said, "…those who are unwilling to acknowledge Me before men." You are actually denying Jesus when you are unwilling to walk in His words. Again, this can be on however small a level you would like to choose, or this could be as grand as you would like to make it. When we hear what He is saying and we do not have a corresponding doing of what He is saying…we deny Him.

I encourage you to be a doer of the word. I encourage you to not only hear what it is that Jesus is saying, but to step into the words and put them into practice. Let it not be said of you that you were unwilling to accept what Jesus was saying and so you decided to no longer walk with Him because of it. The only way to walk with Jesus is to walk in His words; He is the Word personified, remember. Also, it is important to point out that those who turned from Him were called His disciples. These were not just random people that were standing by the side of the

When we hear what He is saying and we do not have a corresponding doing of what He is saying… we deny Him.

road and happened to be listening that day; they were people that at one point were committed.

Allegiance to Jesus means everything. Our allegiance is expressed by our life aligning with His words. We must be committed to what He is saying to us. Regardless of the cost, Jesus is looking for a people that would be willing to acknowledge Him. I don't know if you are aware of it or not, but we are living in days where there is a price to pay for being willing to acknowledge yourself with the real Jesus. I say the real Jesus because the only real Jesus is the one that reflects all of His words. Not everyone is excited about who Jesus is and the things that He said, and in fact, there are those who are losing their very life for the choice of acknowledging this Jesus and being unwilling to deny Him. If you choose to align your life with this Jesus, you will have to count the cost...and even with a great price, I strongly encourage you to step in!

We must not be ashamed of what Jesus has said. We must not back down on the words of Jesus just because they are not received well. We must not modify what He said in order to grow a following for Him. Jesus is fully committed to His words, and He wants you and me to be also. He is fully committed to what He has said, and He is fully committed to what He is saying to you right now.

The revelation of Jesus to a people is dependent on your stepping in to what He is saying. What are you waiting for? Your time is now. Your day is today. Put action to it. Do something about it!

Please take a few moments to watch this stirring
video from one of today's most prominent
and powerful voices.

"The Cost of Discipleship"

https://vimeo.com/122181671

11

Why Not Me?
Why Not Now?

———⊶⊷———

"Every man dies, not every man really lives."
—William Wallace[149]

What will history have to say about you? What is God currently writing about you in this great Kingdom narrative that is continually moving forward and unfolding? What is the vision of your life that is being worked out in the earth to further and fulfill this amazing work that all of creation and time have been steering towards at the end of all things? We have to live with and for a vision that is bigger than our life.

---

[149] "William Wallace – 'Every Man Dies, Not Every Man Really Lives,'" Scotland Welcomes You, http://scotlandwelcomesyou.com/william-wallace/.

God gives vision. If we claim to walk with God we must trust that God is able to fill our lives with vision.

Vision that comes from God empowers a man to realize that there is something, and Someone, much grander to live for than himself.

Vision that comes from God empowers a man to realize that there is something, and Someone, much grander to live for than himself. Many throughout the Scriptures seemed to have their life interrupted in a moment when God stepped in and installed into them a vision much larger than their current life.

Abraham, Moses, Mary, Paul, and many more had a moment with God that reshaped the rest of their days. Many throughout the Scriptures had an encounter with God that caused them to switch lanes and begin living out the reality of things that had been revealed to them by God. As believers, as those who claim to walk with Jesus, it is a necessity that we have an infusion of vision from the Father in our lives.

Why is vision so important? Vision is what allows me to look up and to look out. What do I mean? What I mean is this. Vision is what allows me to see beyond the moment. Vision is what gives me the ability to look up and out beyond the natural, or circumstantial, things that I may be engaged in or connected to at any given moment in time. Vision is what tells me that there is more to life than just what my current experience may be.

Vision fuels hope. Without vision there cannot be hope. Vision is what opens my eyes to the hope that this is not all. Vision is what allows me to believe, and not in a superficial way, but really, that my "what is" is not all that there is to my "what will be."

Vision is what speaks to me when I am down and out and feel like throwing in the towel to say, "Don't quit. There's more for you." Vision is what whispers softly in the moments that life and all of my experiences are screaming that things will never change to say, "Keep going; you're heading in the right direction." Vision allows hope in my life to live and to be revived. Vision will be the voice in your life that comes at a time when possibly every other voice of influence around you is telling you that it is impossible, it will never be, or you should give it up because it will definitely not work out for you, to say, "I am with you, and together, we can do this!"

> **Vision is what allows me to believe...that my "what is" is not all that there is to my "what will be."**

The Father will always return to you the things that He has said to you. He will always bring you back to the things that He has revealed to you. This is another reason that it is a life and death matter that we learn to recognize the still, small voice of the Shepherd, because He truly desires to lead our lives. Without the recognition of this voice we will continually give ourselves to other voices, and then as a natural byproduct of that, be led by others.

When we lack a vision we become a prisoner to our immediate. Without a vision we become captive to the moment. Without a vision there is nothing for us to hope for, or believe for, in the area of change. Without a vision we become a manager of the moment, doing whatever we can day to day just to get by. Being a manager of the moment, we can weary ourselves just trying to survive every day and make it through.

A life that is lived without vision is more prone to be given over to the tendency of feeling as if its life is being wasted, the feeling as if its immediate efforts are not building toward a greater purpose.

We are not supposed to live our lives simply surviving every day. We are not to be those that are given over to just running out the clock daily because life does not seem to have a larger purpose than the routine things that unfold in our life day to day. There is more to live for than just the moment.

A life that is lived without vision is easily shackled to things like hopelessness, despair, and depression because it does not have eyes to see beyond the right now. A life that is lived without vision is more prone to be given over to the tendency of feeling as if its life is being wasted, the feeling as if its immediate efforts are not building toward a greater purpose. A life with no vision, in order to feel successful, will give itself to whatever temporal things in the moment that can be built, even if there is no lasting significance, in order to pacify the relentless internal wrestling that causes us to want to believe our life should matter.

So without continuing the point, needless to say, it is vitally important that our lives are charged with a vision from God. And sometimes the vision that we have in place in our life needs to be challenged, because honestly, at times, we settle for less than what God really has in mind to do. It has been said that the greatest enemy of something great is something good. Good things are at times, the enemy of God things.

What do I mean? Let's take a look at Abram in Genesis chapter 15 in order to find out what all of this is about. Abram is in a place where he is challenged to really believe what it is that God is saying to him about his life. Abram is in a place where all of his natural means have no way to add up to what it is that God has revealed to him that He wants to do in his life. There is no way for Abram to get to what God is saying without God intervening somehow and connecting the dots. What an amazing place to be: fully dependent on God, completely reliant, totally abandoned!

In the opening of Genesis chapter 15 the word of the Lord comes to Abram in a vision (he's not yet Abraham; this happens a little bit later in his life), saying, "Do not be afraid, Abram. I am your shield, your exceedingly great reward."[150] Abram's response seems a little strange when you consider the statement that God just gave him in the vision, Abram says this, "'O Lord GOD, what will You give me, since I am childless, and the heir of my house is Eliezer of Damascus?' And Abram said, 'Since You have given no offspring to me, one born in my house is my heir.'"[151] The things that God has spoken to Abram are obviously on Abram's heart and mind; he is looking at his life and trying to put the pieces together for how God can bring about the promised outcome by what he naturally sees as pieces to work with. Abram cannot make sense of what God has said with what it is that he sees.

God is quick to give Abram a chance to change his perspective. In the next verse God answers Abram's

---

[150] Gen. 15:1, NKJV
[151] Gen. 15:2-3, NASB

objection by saying, "This man will not be your heir; but one who will come forth from your own body, he shall be your heir."[152] Then the Bible gives us an amazing statement that we will unpack for its application to you and me today as we also walk with God and are challenged to believe what God has said in the midst of the limitations that we see in our natural resources and abilities. Verse 5 of Genesis says this, "And He took him outside and said, 'Now look toward the heavens, and count the stars, if you are able to count them.' And He said to him, 'So shall your descendants be.'" It is at this point that the Bible tells us, in verse 6, that Abram believed in the Lord and He reckoned it to him as righteousness.[153]

There are a few quick things that are important to note as we continue so that you can fully appreciate what God is doing for Abram. One is where Abram would have been whenever God spoke to him and asked him to step outside. Abram was traveling, so he would have been set up in a tent. Why is this important? It is important for many reasons, but the one that we will mention is this: the ceiling was too low. The ceiling on the type of tent that Abram would have had would have been a low ceiling. It's a tent, after all, and if you've ever been camping or spent the night in

---

152 Gen. 15:4, NASB
153 Gen. 15:5-6, NASB

a tent, you know that in even the nicest of tents, the ceiling is low.

The issue with a low ceiling is that it challenges our capacity to be able to look up and look out. A low ceiling will cause us to feel boxed in. A low ceiling can make you feel as if there is not a lot of room to grow up and grow into. A low ceiling, in Abram's case, is something that God was specifically speaking to when giving Abram the opportunity to step outside.

There will be moments and seasons in your life where God will speak to you and ask you to step outside. There will be seasons, where in order for Him to accomplish what He is trying to do in your heart and life, you will have to make the decision to step out and away from a low ceiling in your life. There will be significant opportunities that God will present you with to make a clean break from the low capacity, or the inability to believe beyond a certain point in your life.

There will be significant opportunities that God will present you with to make a clean break from the low capacity, or the inability to believe beyond a certain point in your life.

It is also important to note that Abram would not have been alone as he sat in the tent. There would have been other people surrounding him and traveling with him on this journey that God had them on. Why does this matter, or what makes this worthy to mention? In the opportunity to step outside is also the invitation to step away from other voices. The invitation was given to Abram to step away from other voices, and this has profound meaning for you and me as we consider the invitation that God would present to us as well.

Why would you need to step away from other voices? There could have been voices in Abram's life that would have been speaking things contrary to what God had said to him. Can you think of anybody in your life that at any point has been a discouraging voice? Someone that maybe caused you to believe that a certain thing could not be done? Someone that, though they may love you and say they have your best interests at heart, was a continual stumbling block for you in attempting to really believe the things that God was speaking to you about? The invitation to step outside means these are the voices it is time to separate from so that God can adjust your perspective.

The voices that we allow to speak into our life are not always something we are going to be able to just change in a moment. Maybe you've never noticed it before, but when you spend enough time with people that complain, you begin to complain. When you spend time with people that tend to doubt everything, if you're not careful, you will begin to doubt everything. We are greatly influenced by those that we choose to walk beside in life. It is important to identify who surrounds you and the things that, up until this point, have been an influence on you. You must

You must identify those voices in your life that are causing you to shrink back from really believing God.

identify those voices in your life that are causing you to shrink back from really believing God.

Can you hear it? Can you hear the still, small voice of the Shepherd calling out to you, inviting you to step outside? Sometimes God has to call us outside and tell us to look up. By looking into the vastness of the sky and the beauty of the stars we are reminded of how grand He really is. Sometimes God has to call us outside so that we can be reminded that the world is bigger than the little self-absorbed and self-consumed bubble that it is easy to walk around in.

At times, I need to be challenged to believe for more. At times, I need to be invited outside to have the complacency in my life shaken off. There are moments in my life where I've settled into complaining about what I see with my eyes and I need to be reminded of what God has spoken to me.

There are times where the doubt in my life becomes the dominating voice of influence and I need to be invited outside in order to step into believing God again. Stepping out and away from was much needed for Abram, and also for you and me.

I want you to believe what God has said to you about your life and purpose in the earth. I want you to be challenged to step into destiny. I want you to believe that your time is now. You were hand chosen by God to be alive at this moment in time, not just so that you could run out the clock, but so that your life could make a mark on your generation. I want you to believe that you are the breaking point!

You were hand chosen by God to be alive at this moment in time, not just so that you could run out the clock, but so that your life could make a mark on your generation.

Your life is the point through which God is looking to break into this generation. You have to believe that. You have to know that God is desperately looking for a man or a woman that would let Him in. All throughout my process of writing I could hear the voice of the Holy Spirit, crying out, *"I want in! I want in!"*

We have to realize that God is the One waiting for us; God is waiting for you. He waits for you to finally let Him in, not in the little comfortable ways that you have up until this point in your life, but in a way that you can no longer manage. God is waiting for the day that you seriously relinquish control and just go all in!

Jesus wants to change His image, the perspective of who He is and what He is about in the region that you live. Will you be one that stands up in your day to represent Him well? Are you one that is willing to identify with Him in the way that He desires to be revealed?

Again, He can't change a region until He first changes the heart of a man or woman. He can't change a church until He changes the heart of a man or a woman. He can't change a household until He first changes the heart of a man or a woman. He can't change a school campus until He first changes the heart of a man or a woman. He can't change a workplace until He changes the heart of a man or a woman.

God has a greater desire than you to see things changed, but that change rests upon the availability and access of the hearts of His people.

God has a greater desire than you to see things changed, but that change rests upon the availability and access of the hearts of His people. Put your hand over your heart and say this out loud: Before He can break in there, He must break in here!

Stop and take a moment to honestly ask yourself these two questions: Why not me? Why not now? Okay, now this time with a greater amount of confidence: Why not me? Why not now? Why couldn't God use you? Why couldn't your time be right now? God can use you! Your time is right now!

The great cloud of witnesses spoken about in the book of Hebrews chapter 11 is standing, waiting, watching, and cheering you on. All of history has built up to this moment that is before you. What will you do with the day that has been entrusted to you? What will you do in order to give your life meaning and make it count? I can assure you that there is no greater thing in all of the world that you could possibly find to do that would outweigh the significance of wholeheartedly giving yourself to Jesus and the Father's business!

Jesus wants to continue what He Himself came and started, with you. You are the point of penetration for the next move of God. You are the place of access for God to get in. Your life is the point through which God is looking to break into a generation. You are the breaking point!

Please take a few moments to watch this stirring
video from one of today's most prominent
and powerful voices:

"The Emerging of the Jesus People"

https://vimeo.com/122181760

About the Author

Michael is the Founding Director of Burning Ones. At the age of twenty-one Michael was a drug addict, dealer, diseased, and hopeless. It was at this time that he had an encounter with Jesus that radically changed his life. From this point forward he has been relentless in his pursuit of the God-Man, Jesus Christ. Michael now preaches Jesus around the world powerfully with great demonstrations of signs and miracles.

You can find out more about Burning Ones
by visiting:

www.burningones.org
www.facebook.com/burningonesinternational

More about Michael:

www.facebook.com/michaelsdow
www.twitter.com/michaeldow
www.instagram.com/michaeldow

About the Ministry

_⸎

Burning Ones is the ministry of Michael and Anna Dow. Our vision is to raise up burning ones that will make Jesus famous among the nations of the world. We do that by preaching the Gospel of the Kingdom until the hearts of men and women come alive to God and burn with passion for His Son, Jesus, by the power of the Holy Spirit. We preach Jesus in church services, conferences, and mass crusades around the world with extraordinary signs and miracles.

When He consumes our lives, we become His burning ones! We are burning ones by experience and expression. We experience Him and then we express Him to the world. Burning Ones is not something that is exclusive for us to a specific time and space; it is life itself!

Website: www.burningones.org
Facebook: burningonesinternational
E-mail: info@burningones.org

FREE INDEED

Does God have to have your agreement in order for Him to have your obedience? Will you obey the call of God even if there is not an instant payout or benefit to you? Many are willing to step into obedience and do what God is asking so long as they are the primary beneficiaries of their obedience. Are you willing to walk with a God that you cannot control? Can you handle walking with a Jesus that you cannot manipulate and leverage your faithfulness against? There is a confrontation that awaits you in the text...a confrontation to determine what kind of Jesus follower you are going to be. In the book *Free Indeed*, Michael challenges the reader to surrender everything to Jesus and invest the rest of their life into uncompromised obedience to Him.

Available at:

Amazon

Kindle

iBooks

www.burningones.org